England
A Very
Peculiar
History™

Volume 3

'There is a forgotten, nay almost forbidden
word, which means more to me than any other.
That word is England.'

Sir Winston Churchill

Editor: Stephen Haynes
Editorial assistants: Rob Walker, Mark Williams

Published in Great Britain in MMXIII by
Book House, an imprint of
The Salariya Book Company Ltd
25 Marlborough Place, Brighton BN1 1UB
www.salariya.com
www.book-house.co.uk

HB ISBN-13: 978-1-908973-37-5 vol. 1
978-1-908973-38-2 vol. 2
978-1-908973-39-9 vol. 3
978-1-908973-41-2 boxed set

1 3 5 7 9 8 6 4 2

A CIP catalogue record for this book is available
from the British Library.
Printed and bound in Dubai.
Printed on paper from sustainable sources.

Visit
www.salariya.com
for our online catalogue and
free interactive web books.

England
A Very Peculiar History™

Volume 3
From Trafalgar to the
New Elizabethans

By
John Malam

Created and designed by
David Salariya

'On a fine day [the English climate is] like looking up a chimney; on a rainy day it is like looking down it.'
Irish poet Thomas Moore, Diary, 22 May 1828

'Even a boiled egg tastes of mutton fat in England.'
Expatriate British writer Norman Douglas, *Old Calabria*, 1915

'England is the most class-ridden country under the sun. It is a land of snobbery and privilege, ruled largely by the old and silly.'
George Orwell, *England Your England*, 1941

'Fog in Channel – Continent cut off.'
Newspaper headline allegedly used in the 1930s

Contents

Ten things to thank the modern English for

1. **The computer** Where would we be today without computers? The idea for a machine that could be programmed to make calculations dates from the 1820s, when Charles Babbage invented the 'difference engine', the world's first mechanical computer.

2. **Polyester fibre** Poured a drink from a plastic bottle recently? Chances are it was made from polyethylene terephthalate (PET for short), a type of polyester fibre. It was chemist John Rex Whinfield who produced the world's first polyester fibre in 1941, which was put to use in fabrics under the brand name Terylene.

3. **Wind-up radio** This ingenious device, invented in 1989 by Trevor Baylis, doesn't use batteries or mains electricity. A few turns of the handle is all that's needed to make the radio work.

4. **The microchip** In the late 1940s, Geoffrey Dummer, of the Telecommunications Research Establishment at Malvern in Worcestershire, came up with the idea for the integrated circuit, commonly called the microchip. It's at the heart of today's computers and electronic gadgets.

5. **The rubber band** Stephen Perry's useful invention for holding a batch of envelopes together hasn't changed much since he patented his idea in 1845.

6. **The mousetrap** Patented in 1897 by Leeds ironmonger James Henry Atkinson, the 'Little Nipper' snapped shut in 38 thousandths of a second. It is still in production today.

7. **Football** The game has been played in England in some form or other since medieval times (see Vol. 1, page 17). True, footballs may have been kicked around in other countries, but what matters is where the modern rules of football come from, and that's Cambridge University in 1848.

8. **The safety bicycle** The world's first modern bike was invented in 1885 by John Starley of Coventry. His two-wheeled invention is still keeping people on the move, worldwide.

9. **The jet engine** Another famous Coventrian (person from Coventry) was Sir Frank Whittle, inventor of the jet engine in the 1930s. It powers today's fighter planes, airliners and freight planes.

10. **The sandwich** Really? John Montagu, 4th Earl of Sandwich, may not have invented the humble sandwich... but he did give it its name in the 1700s!

Putting modern England on the map

1. Westhoughton Mill, near Bolton, attacked by Luddites and set on fire, 1812
2. Spa Fields Riot, London, 1816: a failed attempt to start an English Revolution
3. Peterloo Massacre, Manchester, 1819: protest meeting broken up by cavalry – 11 dead
4. Swing Riots, 1830–1831: agricultural protests begin in Kent and spread throughout the south
5. Stockton & Darlington Railway, 1825: world's first steam-powered public railway
6. Liverpool & Manchester Railway, 1830: world's first passenger railway
7. Tolpuddle, Dorset, 1834: six farm workers transported for forming a trade union
8. Cambridge, 1848: first rules of football drawn up
9. Great Exhibition, London, 1851
10. Broad Street cholera outbreak, London, 1854: cholera shown to be caused by polluted water
11. Epsom, 1913: suffragette Emily Davison killed
12. Scarborough, Whitby and Hartlepool bombarded by German battleships, 1914
13. Zeppelins attack Great Yarmouth and King's Lynn, 1915
14. Jarrow, 1936: unemployed workers march to London to highlight unemployment
15. Festival of Britain, London, 1951
16. Wembley Stadium, London, 1966: England win the football World Cup
17. Orgreave, Yorkshire: mounted police charge at striking miners, 1984
18. London hosts the Olympic Games three times: 1908, 1948, 2012

Green and pleasant?
Britain becomes the first
industrial nation

ENGLAND, THIS ENGLAND

How can the story of England during the last two centuries be told? The short answer is that the 19th century was the period when England punched above its weight to become a world superpower, only to see it slip away in the 20th century. For the longer answer, read on.

Let's start by clearing up the sometimes confusing issue of political geography. Although this book is about the country known as England, and the people of that country, called the English, the story of the last 200 or so years cannot be told without mentioning Great Britain, or Britain for short. 'Britain' can mean two things. First, it is the name of a large island off the northwest coast of continental Europe (that should deal with the geography issue). Second, Britain is the collective name given to the three countries that occupy the island of the same name. Those countries are England (the biggest of the three), Scotland and Wales (and that's the political bit).*

It's important to be clear about this from the start, as it will be unavoidable at times to take England and the English out of Britain and the British for the period in question. For example, the British Empire was exactly that – an overseas empire controlled by Britain; the World War II air battle fought over the skies of southern England has gone down in history as the Battle of Britain (only in Germany is it known as the *Luftschlacht um England*, the 'air battle for England'); and the

* *The nearby island of Ireland is not part of Great Britain, though Great Britain and Ireland together are referred to as the British Isles. From 1801 to 1922, Ireland was part of the United Kingdom of Great Britain and Ireland. Today, Northern Ireland is part of the United Kingdom of Great Britain and Northern Ireland; the rest of the island of Ireland forms the independent Republic of Ireland.*

Festival of Britain (1951) was a national showcase of British achievements which happened to have its main exhibition site in London, England.

The 19th and 20th centuries were times of non-stop change, when England faced both good times and bad times. On the one hand it was a time of invention, innovation, growth and prosperity for England; but, in stark contrast, there were also times of hardship, unrest and conflict. Of course, the same can be said for earlier periods in England's long and glorious history, but in the years since 1800 the nation's highs seem to have scaled greater heights than ever before, and the lows have seemingly plumbed new depths.

Shoulder to shoulder

When the political map of Britain was drawn up centuries ago, setting out the boundaries of England, Scotland and Wales, England's share worked out at a little more than 50,000 square miles (130,000 km^2), which is roughly the size it is today. For comparison with other territories around the world, this makes

England about the same size as Greece, or the US state of Mississippi. But that's where the comparison ends, because into this small area is squeezed a population of 53 million people, making England one of the most crowded countries in Europe, with some 407 people for every square kilometre of land (Holland tops the list with 494, and Greece is way down with a mere 87).

So how did little England end up with such an enormous population? A glance at the census figures shows how the population has kept on rising since the first modern survey in 1801 (you have to go back to the Domesday Book of 1086 for the nation's earliest headcount).

Year	Population
1801	8,308,000
1811	9,496,000
1821	11,158,000
1831	12,993,000
1841	14,866,000
1851	16,769,400
1861	18,776,300
1871	21,298,000
1881	24,402,700

1891	27,231,200
1901	30,515,000
1911	33,651,600
1921	35,230,200
1931	37,359,000
1941	*no census*
1951	41,042,200
1961	43,983,300
1971	45,870,100
1981	46,623,500
1991	48,067,300
2001	49,138,831
2011	53,012,456

Will the population of England continue to rise? According to the Office of National Statistics, whose job is to forecast trends, this is what's to come:

Year	*Population*
2015	54.5 million
2020	56.6 million
2025	58.6 million
2030	60.4 million
2035	62.1 million

Land of hope and glory

Periods in history are usually remembered for famous people (good ones and bad ones), and for significant events. England in the 19th and 20th centuries can be recalled not only for its leaders, reformers, inventors, pioneers and campaigners, but also for the silent majority – that ever-expanding population – who, in the phrases of the day, played their part in building an 'empire on which the sun never sets', in forging the 'workshop of the world', in fighting 'the war to end all wars', and in 'digging for victory'.

Prime ministers promised them 'a land fit for heroes' (David Lloyd George, 1918), told them they had 'never had it so good' (Harold Macmillan, 1957), and that the country was going to be rebuilt in the 'white heat of technology' (Harold Wilson, 1963). The flipside included the 'Winter of Discontent' (1978–1979), a prime minister proclaiming 'There is no such thing as society' (Margaret Thatcher, 1987) and a time of austerity and recession brought on by the worldwide 'credit crunch' which reached these shores in 2007.

So, the last 200 years have been something of a roller-coaster ride for England, this England. But, despite the ups and downs, as the encouraging words of the well-known patriotic song put it, this is a 'land of hope and glory'. In fact, there are many in England who would like to see 'Land of Hope and Glory' become the country's official national anthem, since England doesn't actually have one (no, it's not 'God Save the Queen', which is the national anthem for the whole of the United Kingdom, not just England).

Another candidate for England's national anthem is the much-loved song-cum-hymn known as 'Jerusalem', which appeals to English flag-waving pride. Written as a poem by William Blake in 1808 (the familiar rousing tune by Sir Hubert Parry only came along in 1916), it gave us those contrasting phrases 'England's green and pleasant land' and 'dark Satanic mills'.

And that is where this story of England's recent past can begin, as a nation on the brink of transforming itself from agriculture to industry, from farms to factories.

Left to right: dragoon, hussar, Polish lancer

Invasion force:
Bonaparte expected his
Grande Armée to make short
work of Britain's defences

CHAPTER ONE

RESTLESS ENGLAND

The word on everyone's mind as the 18th century came to an end was 'revolution'. It was a word that struck fear into governments and monarchies as ordinary people rose up against their leaders and took control away from them. And so it was that in 1783 America broke away from Britain in the American Revolution, and the United States of America was born. As if losing this overseas colony wasn't bad enough, around the same time France had a revolution, then decided to invade England – but things didn't go to plan.

Here comes the bogeyman

On a clear day the White Cliffs of Dover, on the southeast coast of England, can be seen from France across the English Channel. It's a short distance of about 21 miles (34 km), and this narrow stretch of sea is all that keeps England, and the island of Britain, from being joined to the continent of Europe.

In 1803 a French general planned to invade England by sending a large army across the English Channel. The army was called the *Armée de l'Angleterre* (Army of England), and the general was Napoleon Bonaparte. His ambition was to make England part of his growing European empire.

The English had a nickname for Bonaparte: they called him 'Boney'. Such was Bonaparte's scary reputation that his name was used in an English nursery rhyme of the time. Some suggest that 'Boney' is where we get the words 'bogey' and 'bogeyman' from. English children must have been scared to close their eyes at night after their parents recited this rhyme to them:

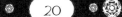

Baby, baby, naughty baby,
Hush! you squalling thing, I say;
Peace this instant! Peace! or maybe
Bonaparte will pass this way.

Baby, baby, he's a giant,
Tall and black as Rouen steeple,
Sups and dines and lives reliant
Every day on naughty people.

Baby, baby, if he hears you
As he gallops past the house,
Limb from limb at once he'll tear you,
Just as pussy tears a mouse.

And he'll beat you, beat you, beat you,
And he'll beat you all to pap,
And he'll eat you, eat you, eat you,
Every morsel – snap! snap! snap!

Napoleon Bonaparte certainly intended to
'pass this way' – to invade England – and the
English knew that very well.

He's coming to get you!
An idealised portrait
of Napoleon Bonaparte
at the head of his army

The invasion that never was

Bonaparte had risen to power in France and had become the country's leader. But his ambitions didn't stop there. He wanted to become the ruler of all Europe, and in 1797 he made an announcement that sent shivers down English spines. He said:

> Our government must destroy the English monarchy, or expect itself to be destroyed by these intriguing and enterprising islanders . . . Let us concentrate all our efforts on the navy and annihilate England. That done, Europe is at our feet.

His intentions couldn't have been clearer, and in 1803 Britain declared war on France, embarking on what became known as the Napoleonic Wars.

Bonaparte insulted England as a 'nation of shopkeepers', implying that the country would be easy to defeat. He assembled a massive invasion force along the northern coast of France (accounts vary between 130,000 and 200,000 men). While his Army of England

waited for orders to board the 2,000 barges that were to carry them across the English Channel, they trained, waited, and got bored.

Meanwhile, England got ready to repel the invaders. Along the south coast, defences were strengthened. Martello towers were built, Dover Castle had underground tunnels added to house extra troops, and the Royal Military Canal was cut to slow the French invaders down, should they come ashore in the area of Romney Marsh, Kent.

Martello towers

- **What were they?** Small, round forts. They were built of stone with walls 13 ft (4 m) thick, stood about 30 ft (9 m) high and were armed with a long-range 24-pounder cannon on the flat roof, pointing out to sea. Inside were rooms where a unit of 24 men and an officer lived.

- **Where were they?** Along the coasts of Sussex, Kent, Essex and Suffolk.

- **How many were built?** 103, between 1805 and 1812.

- **Were they ever used in action?** No.

Rumours spread that the French army would sail across the English Channel on a gigantic raft powered by windmills and paddlewheels (as if!), or that soldiers would march along a secret tunnel dug under the sea (an idea ahead of its time), or they would be blown across in an invasion fleet of balloons (believe it or not, Bonaparte really did think about using balloons, but gave up on the idea).

Bonaparte knew only too well that the key to success lay in controlling the English Channel. He is supposed to have said: 'Let us be masters of the Channel for six hours, and we are masters of the world.' Six hours is all he thought he would need to move his Army of England across the ribbon of choppy sea that separates France from England. Six hours, and he'd be setting foot in England.

Before the full-scale invasion of England went ahead, the French tested out their barges. It was a complete disaster: the troop-carriers were badly built and not up to the job. Bonaparte was forced to think again, and in the summer of 1805 he turned his attention elsewhere. The Army of England was

renamed the *Grande Armée* ('Great Army'), and off it marched to set about conquering much of mainland Europe. The French plan to invade England was called off.

Rule, Britannia!

Could England now relax? Not at all! The country was still at war with France, and on 21 October 1805 the Royal Navy faced the combined fleets of the French and Spanish navies in the Battle of Trafalgar, fought a few miles off the southwest coast of Spain.

In charge of the Royal Navy warships was Admiral Lord Horatio Nelson, on board HMS *Victory*. At 11.45 a.m. Nelson sent his famous message to the fleet: 'England expects that every man will do his duty.'

The British ships advanced in two columns to break the enemy's line of battle; this manoeuvre made the leading ships dangerously exposed. The first shots were fired at about midday. For five hours the roar of cannons was heard for miles around, and when at last their thunder fell silent, Nelson's victory over the French was complete. The Royal Navy was now the world's supreme naval power, and Britain ruled the waves.

Tragically, Nelson didn't make it home alive. He was shot at close range by a French marksman and died three hours after the bullet ripped through him. His body was preserved in a barrel of brandy mixed with camphor and myrrh; this was then lashed to the *Victory*'s mainmast for the journey back to England, where Nelson was laid to rest in St Paul's Cathedral, London.

Some years later a public square was built in London to commemorate the battle. And towering over Trafalgar Square is Nelson's Column – a 145 ft (44 m) tribute to a national war hero.

Trafalgar statistics

Date: 21 October 1805
Location: Cape Trafalgar, Spain

Number of ships

Royal Navy:	33
France:	26
Spain:	15

Ships captured or lost

Royal Navy:	0
France:	10 captured, 1 lost
Spain:	11 captured

Casualties

Royal Navy:	458 killed
	1,208 wounded
France:	2,218 killed
	1,155 wounded
Spain:	1,025 killed
	1,383 wounded

Result: Decisive British victory

Victory at Waterloo

The war at sea may have ended, but Napoleon Bonaparte's plans for control of Europe carried on. By 1809 his empire stretched from Portugal in the west to the borders of Russia in the east. But in 1812 his Great Army was forced to retreat from Russia. Thousands died on the long, cold march back to France, and Bonaparte's days were numbered.

His end came on 18 June 1815, near Waterloo in Belgium, when he was defeated by a coalition British and Prussian army. In charge of the British troops was Arthur Wellesley, Duke of Wellington. A national war hero, he gave his name to the Wellington boot – a new type of high boot which he commissioned.

The Battle of Waterloo was a turning point for Europe. It brought to an end 23 years of war which had started in France in 1792. The victory at Waterloo left Britain as the leading power in Europe. Had the battle gone differently, Bonaparte might well have crossed the English Channel at the head of an invading French army.

Waterloo statistics

Date: 18 June 1815
Location: Waterloo, Belgium

Number of combatants

British:	68,000
Prussian:	50,000
French:	72,000

Number of cannons

British:	160
Prussian:	126
French:	250

Casualties

British:	3,500 killed
	10,200 wounded
Prussian:	1,200 killed
	4,400 wounded
French:	25,000 killed
	and wounded

Result: Decisive victory for
the British–Prussian
coalition

Ten things you didn't know about the Battle of Waterloo

1. The battle lasted all day, from about 11.30 a.m. until about 8.00 p.m.

2. The average age of British soldiers was 23. Most had been farm labourers before enlisting in the army. They were paid one shilling per day.

3. The Royal Dragoons captured the bronze eagle of the French 105th regiment and adopted it as their badge. The regiment was nicknamed 'the Bird Catchers'.

4. A French cannonball struck the Earl of Uxbridge as he rode with the Duke of Wellington. The Duke said, 'By God, you've lost your leg.' The Earl replied, 'By God, so I have.' The remains of the leg were amputated in a house nearby and the owner buried the leg in his garden.

5. Prussian general Blücher wanted to name the battle *La Belle Alliance* (The Beautiful Alliance) in recognition of the countries that had fought Bonaparte. But this was also the name of Bonaparte's command post, and Wellington refused to name the battle after the loser's headquarters! Instead, he named it after the small town where he had spent the night before the battle – Waterloo.

6. Bonaparte suffered from haemorrhoids (piles) and his doctor used leeches to reduce the pain. During the night of 16 June the leeches were lost, so his doctor gave him a strong dose of laudanum, which left him feeling groggy and not fit for battle!

7. Heavy rain helped the Duke of Wellington win the battle. The French guns sank up to their axles in mud and their cavalry could not charge uphill on the soggy ground. The start of the battle was delayed by two hours, so the ground could dry out a little.

8. Bonaparte said he had lost at Waterloo because of the 'obstinate and unyielding bravery of the English troops'. In fact, there were more Irish than English in the British army.

9. The French footsoldiers moved about the battlefield in columns, whereas the British fought in thin lines, two men deep.

10. In 2012, the skeleton of a soldier killed at Waterloo was found buried on the battlefield. He'd been shot, and the lead musket ball that had killed him was found in his ribcage. He was a British soldier aged about 20, and buried with him was a piece of wood with the letters CB on it – probably his initials.

The machine-breakers

The early 1800s were a time of restlessness and conflict. There had recently been revolutions in America and France, which were political in origin, but England was in the grip of a different kind of revolution – one of the greatest social upheavals the nation had ever known. This was the Industrial Revolution, in which the country's traditional farming economy was being rapidly transformed into one based on manufacturing and machines. It was changing the way things were made and how people worked.

One of the first sectors to be revolutionised was the textile industry, where machines were brought in to do the work that used to be done by hand. Machines were fast, they worked non-stop, and they put people out of work.

In England's textile towns of Lancashire, Yorkshire, Nottinghamshire, Leicestershire and Derbyshire, machines were seen as enemies of the textile workers. Faced with unemployment and starvation, weavers, spinners and others took direct action.

Between 1811 and 1816, groups met in secret and swore oaths to destroy the machines that were threatening their way of life. They were known as Luddites, named after their imaginary leader 'General Ned Ludd' who, like the English folk-hero Robin Hood, was said to live in Sherwood Forest, Nottinghamshire.

Under cover of darkness, Luddites smashed machines and set factories ablaze. Posters offered rewards for information leading to their arrest, spies were set to work, and the government put 12,000 troops onto the streets of the worst affected towns. But, after each attack, the machine-breakers disappeared back into the safety of their communities.

Despite their actions, the Luddites were fighting a losing battle. They couldn't stop industrial progress – machines were here to stay. The government got tough and in 1812 introduced the death penalty for anyone found guilty of machine-breaking. Those Luddites who did escape the hangman's noose were transported to serve long sentences in the penal colonies of Australia.

Luddite attack on Westhoughton Mill

Date:	Friday 24 April 1812
Location:	Westhoughton Mill, Bolton, Lancashire
What happened?	Luddites burned the mill down.
Any security?	Army guards had left for the weekend.
Arrests:	24
Hanged:	Abraham Charlson, 16 Job Fletcher, 34 Thomas Kerfoot, 26 James Smith, 31
Transported:	12 men shipped off to Australia for 7 years

Abraham Charlson, the youngest of the condemned, was little more than a boy. His family claimed he was 12, not 16, and was too young to be hanged. The judge disagreed, and on 13 June 1812 Charlson and the other three Luddites were hanged at Lancaster Castle, in front of a large crowd of onlookers.

Peace brings unrest

In 1815 the Napoleonic Wars ended after 20 years, and in the following year the Luddite protests fizzled out. But, instead of things getting back to normal in peacetime, the opposite happened.

The war had kept England's factories and workshops busy making everything the army needed, and farmers had done their bit for the war effort by ploughing up more land to feed the population.

The war with France had given a boost to the economy and kept people in work. It had been a time of growth and prosperity, but when peace came, boom turned to bust and England entered a period of depression and gloom.

Factories produced fewer goods, profits slumped, and workers lost their jobs. With no war to fight, the army and navy needed fewer men. Thousands of soldiers and sailors left the armed forces and returned home, and with little work to be had they added to the growing ranks of the unemployed.

The situation was no better for farmers. During the war England was starved of corn from Europe – Bonaparte had put a stop to supplies of wheat, barley and oats from across the Channel. The result was that home-grown corn went up in price. Then, when the war ended, supplies of cheap corn reached England again – and the price fell.

Farmers protested that imported cheap corn would ruin them. The government stepped in by passing the Corn Laws, which were designed to keep the price of corn high.

There were two problems with the government's price-fixing scheme. First, high corn prices led to high bread prices and, for people who were out of work or on low incomes, this was a big concern. Second, there was a feeling that Members of Parliament (MPs) had put their own interests first. Why? Because most MPs were landowners, or came from wealthy land-owning families, so it was in their interests to keep the price of corn high. By fixing the price, the land-owning MPs were getting richer at the expense of the poor. It was a recipe for unrest.

Farm-workers demanded higher wages and a fixed maximum price for bread. They set fire to barns and hay ricks, and smashed machinery. Weavers, coalminers and factory workers protested against rising prices and unemployment, and called on the government to do something. There were riots across the country.

Spa fields riot

- **When?** 2 December 1816

- **Where?** Spa Fields, Islington, London

- **What?** A mass uprising of the working classes, who planned to seize the Tower of London and the Bank of England and overthrow the government.

- **Why?** They hoped to start an English revolution, just as the French mob had stormed the Bastille fortress in Paris in 1789 and overthrown their leaders.

- **So what happened?** The government knew about the plan all along because a spy was keeping them well informed. They sent in the troops to disperse the crowd, and arrested the ringleaders.

The failed uprising at Spa Fields, London, unsettled the government. It was a sign of how much discontent there was amongst workers. Demonstrations continued. A march on the city of Nottingham, planned for 9 June 1817, was broken up by the cavalry before it could start, and the ringleaders were executed.

Jeremiah Brandreth

- **Born:** Wilford, Nottinghamshire, between 1786 and 1790

- **Known as:** The Nottingham Captain

- **Occupation:** Stockinger – a person who knits stockings (long socks) on a stocking frame

- **Activism:** He may have been a Luddite, breaking textile machines in 1811. On 9 June 1817 he organised a march on Nottingham to overthrow the government and end poverty.

- **Executed:** Found guilty with two others of high treason. Hanged in public at Derby, 7 November 1817. Once dead, his head was chopped off with an axe – the last time a condemned man was beheaded in Britain.

The Peterloo Massacre

The years of workers' unrest continued, coming to a dreadful climax in Manchester on Monday 16 August 1819.

It was a glorious summer's day, and groups of people from Manchester and surrounding towns made their way peacefully and in good spirits to an open area of land known as St Peter's Field. Many of the workmen were dressed in their Sunday best clothes and had brought their wives and children with them for a day out. They carried banners, some of which read 'Reform', 'Unity and Strength', 'Love' and 'Equal Representation'.

An estimated 50,000 people gathered in an orderly manner to hear a speech by the radical politician Henry Hunt, known as 'Orator Hunt' because of his skill at public speaking. Hunt was a supporter of the working class, and he was expected to speak out against poverty, rising food prices and the political system that gave power to the rich – the working poor did not even have the right to vote in elections.

Watching from nearby buildings were Manchester's magistrates – the town's law enforcers. Fearing a riot, they ordered Hunt's arrest. This is what happened next:

- The local yeomanry (part-time soldiers), who may have been drunk, went into the crowd on horseback, armed with swords and clubs. Some had old scores to settle and lashed out at people they recognised.

- The crowd closed in around the yeomanry, protecting Hunt and preventing his arrest.

- Thinking the yeomanry was under attack, the magistrates panicked and sent in the regular troops with orders to disperse the crowd.

- At 1.50 p.m. the 15th Hussars charged, as if fighting an enemy regiment.

- It took just ten minutes for the cavalry to scatter the crowd, leaving 11 unarmed men, women and children dead, cut through by swords and trampled by horses. The youngest was 2 years old. Hundreds were injured.

- Working people called the massacre at St Peter's Field 'Peterloo', as a mocking comparison with the Battle of Waterloo.

The Peterloo Massacre drew protests from all classes of society, and the government faced mounting criticism calling for the political system to be reformed.

Did the government listen? No! Instead, 10,000 more soldiers were recruited to the army and tough new laws were swiftly passed (the Six Acts, 1819) which gave magistrates powers to search people and houses for weapons, forbidden newspapers and pamphlets, and to sentence offenders without a judge-and-jury trial. The new laws also banned meetings of 50 or more people.

Cato Street conspiracy

On 23 February 1820 a group of revolutionaries met at a house in Cato Street, London. They planned to assassinate the Cabinet and start an 'English Republic'. But amongst them was a government spy. Soldiers and Bow Street Runners (police officers) arrived and the gang was arrested. Four were hanged at Newgate Gaol, London, 1 May 1820.

Changing the system

After 1820 it wasn't only the working-class poor who were calling for changes to the system. Middle-class doctors, lawyers and factory owners also felt ignored by the government. Something had to be done, and in 1832 the Representation of the People Act (known as the Reform Act) was passed.

The Reform Act was a milestone in British politics. It marked the beginning of true parliamentary democracy in which the country was governed by Members of Parliament who had been elected by ordinary people, not just by privileged, rich landowners.

The Act didn't get everything right, and problems still remained. For example, only men could vote in elections, not women. Although more men now had the right to vote, they had to own a certain amount of property or land – the poorest still couldn't vote.

Despite its failings, the Reform Act was regarded as a step in the right direction, as it put power into the hands of the middle classes.

1832 Reform Act: highlights

- The number of men who could vote in elections increased from 478,000 to 813,000.

- There was a shake-up of seats in the House of Commons, and industrial towns such as Manchester, Liverpool and Sheffield got their own MPs for the first time.

- Half of the 'rotten boroughs' lost their MPs. These were constituencies with only a handful of voters, all under the control of a powerful landowner who could effectively pick the MP he wanted.

By a strange quirk of fate, the Palace of Westminster (the home of the government in London) was accidentally burned to the ground in 1834. Had there been a French invasion or a revolution, the building would have been an obvious target – but it was an overheated stove that did the damage. Out of the ashes rose a new Palace of Westminster, the building known around the world today.

Hard times for the rural poor

The 1830s was a decade of change as the pace of the Industrial Revolution increased (see Chapter 2). Thousands of jobs were being created in the new factories of England's manufacturing towns, drawing workers in from the countryside. For many countryfolk, factory work meant a new start in life and an escape from rural poverty.

Here are some of the reasons why many country people found themselves living below the breadline:

- They had lost their ancient right to graze their sheep on common land, and their pigs could no longer wander through the forest. Landowners put hedges, fences and walls around common land, enclosing it and claiming it as their own.

- They had lost the right to grow food on common land to feed their families.

- They had lost the right to collect fallen timber from forest trees to use as fuel.

As a popular verse from the time put it:

> The law arrests the man or woman
> Who steals the goose from off the common,
> But leaves the greater rascal loose
> Who steals the common from the goose.

The 'greater rascal' was any grasping landowner who seized the common land that the rural poor had used for centuries.

Many country families were reduced to starvation level. William Cobbett, a radical politician, had this to say about the plight of farm labourers in the county of Wiltshire:

> Their dwellings are little better than pig-beds, and their looks indicate that their food is not nearly equal to that of a pig. Their wretched hovels are stuck upon little bits of ground at the road side . . . In my whole life I never saw human wretchedness equal to this.

When farm workers asked for more money, some employers actually cut their wages. In the 1830s, for working 70 hours a week in all weathers, a man might be paid 9 shillings – hardly enough to meet the basic cost of living.

How the other half lived

How they made ends meet in the 1830s

*Farm workers' weekly wages**

Man:	9 shillings
Woman:	9 pence
Son (aged 18):	4 shillings
Son (aged 12):	2 shillings
Son (aged 11):	1 shilling
Son (aged 8):	1 shilling

Basic cost of living each week

Rent:	1 shilling 2 pence
Bread:	9 shillings
Tea:	2 pence
Potatoes:	1 shilling
Sugar:	3½ pence
Darning thread:	2½ pence
Soap:	3 pence
Candles:	3 pence
Salt:	½ penny
Coal and wood:	9 pence
Butter:	4½ pence
Cheese:	3 pence
Total:	13 shillings 9 pence

*1 shilling = 12 pence

Revolting peasants

In the winter of 1830–1831, a movement sprang up in the county of Kent which swept the south of England from East Anglia to Dorset and Devon. It was led by 'Captain Swing', an imaginary character who inspired farm workers just as 'General Ned Ludd' had inspired the Luddites to take action in towns 20 years earlier.

Like the Luddites, farm workers were also concerned over the use of machines – in particular, machines for threshing corn. Their wages were dependent on the corn harvest, and they relied on the winter work of threshing the corn by hand to keep their families from starving. The introduction of the threshing machine meant that this winter work was no longer available, so their wages were cut.

However, unlike the Luddites, who gave no notice when they set off to smash and burn, the followers of Captain Swing sent warning letters to the landowners on whose farms the threshing machines worked:

Sir,

This is to acquaint you that if your thrashing [*sic*] machines are not destroyed by you directly we shall commence our labours. Signed on behalf of the whole.

Swing

Within months, hundreds of threshing machines had been destroyed in what became known as the Swing Riots – the largest rural uprising since the Peasants' Revolt of the 14th century.

The government acted quickly to put an end to the riots, giving local magistrates powers to hand out whatever sentences they thought fit:

- **2,000 people were arrested**

- **644 were sent to prison**

- **500 were transported**

- **252 were sentenced to death (of which 233 had their sentences commuted to transportation for life)**

- **19 were executed by hanging, including a boy of 12.**

The Tolpuddle Martyrs

Tolpuddle is a tiny village in Dorset, in the southwest of England. In 1833, six farm workers from the village formed a trade union, the Tolpuddle Friendly Society of Agricultural Labourers. The men had recently seen their already low wages cut by three shillings a year, leaving them about £20 a year to live on. By uniting under a common cause they hoped their employers would listen to their calls for a fair day's pay. In fact, the opposite happened.

Trade unions had become legal in 1824, and the government was fearful of the power they had to bring workers together. The Tolpuddle six had not broken the law in forming a union, but when they joined it each man took a secret oath – and this was their undoing.

The government wanted to weaken the power of trade unions and put people off joining them, so an example was made of the farm workers from Tolpuddle. In 1834 the men were charged with taking an illegal oath – under a law intended to stop mutiny in the navy. It was a trumped-up, unfair charge.

A Tolpuddle who's who

George Loveless, 37
James Loveless, brother of George, 26
James Brine, 21
Thomas Standfield, 44
John Standfield, son of Thomas, 21
James Hammett, 23

At their trial, George Loveless, the leader of the group, gave this as their defence:

> My Lord, if we have violated any law, it was not done intentionally. We have injured no man's reputation, character, person or property. We were uniting together to preserve ourselves, our wives and our children from utter degradation and starvation. We challenge any man or number of men to prove that we have acted, or intended to act, different from the above statement.

1834: The six were transported for seven years to prison colonies in Australia and Tasmania.

1835–1836: Following protests, the men were pardoned by the government.

1837–1839: The men came home.

1840s: Five of the men emigrated to Canada. Only James Hammett stayed in England.

Help for the poor

Before 1834 there were several ways of providing help for the poor, but that year all the different methods were replaced by one, under the Poor Law Amendment Act.

Parishes were grouped into 'unions' and each one had to build a workhouse. Anyone who wanted help had to go into the workhouse, where conditions were worse than anything outside. Giving money to the poor living in their own homes was banned, unless they were old or sick.

A workhouse recipe

Gruel was a staple workhouse food consisting of cereal boiled in water. It was a thinner version of porridge and was usually served at breakfast.

To make 1 pint of gruel, heat the following in a pan until boiling. Serve with bread.

- 1 pt (0.6 litre) water
- 2 oz (60 g) oatmeal
- ½ oz (15 g) treacle
- pinch of salt

Towards a new era

For all the changes, protests, hardship and unrest during the first three decades of the 19th century, one part of British society remained much the same: the monarchy.

The century began in the reign of King George III (reigned 1760–1820), often unkindly remembered as 'The Mad King' due to his health problems in old age. It's fairer to call him the 'The King Who Lost America', as the American Revolution took place during his long reign.

Regency

George III's declining mental health was cause for concern, and in 1811 he was deemed unfit to rule. His eldest son, George, Prince of Wales, was appointed to rule in his place as regent, which he did for nine years until 1820, when he became king in his own right. This short period, known as the Regency era, is notable for its elegant style and a flourishing of the arts.

Prince of Whales

George III died in 1820 and was succeeded by his son, George IV, whose nickname 'Prince of Whales' is a clue to his bloated size (17 stone 7 pounds, or 111 kg). He'd already been acting king, with the title of Prince Regent, since 1811, due to his father's poor health.

Despite an extravagant lifestyle (too many late nights, too much to eat, and a liking for laudanum), George IV was one of the greatest patrons of art Britain has ever known. He built himself a fantastic holiday home in Brighton, the Royal Pavilion, where he lived in elegance and squalor combined. In its overheated, gas-lit rooms he drank brandy for breakfast, and eventually grew too fat to climb upstairs and had to sleep on the ground floor.

George IV died in 1830 and, as he left no legitimate children, it fell to his younger brother, William, to assume the role of monarch. And on the death of William IV, on 20 June 1837, the crown was passed to his 18-year-old niece, Princess Alexandrina Victoria. The Victorian era had begun.

Stephenson's Rocket
trounced the opposition at
trials held by the Liverpool
and Manchester Railway
in 1829

CHAPTER TWO

WORKSHOP OF THE VICTORIAN WORLD

The nation almost ended up with 'Queen Alexandrina'. Instead, the day after the teenage Alexandrina Victoria became the new monarch of the United Kingdom of Great Britain and Ireland in 1837, she asked to be known by her middle name. And so began the long and glorious reign of Queen Victoria, who, by the 1850s, had given her name to an era: the Victorian age. It was an era that spanned the rest of the century right through to the beginning of the next, and saw Britain emerge as the workshop of the world.

The transport revolution

Queen Victoria came to the throne as the second phase of the Industrial Revolution was underway. The first phase, from the 1750s, had seen the rise of machines and factories, a rapid increase in production, and a doubling of England's population (about 6 million people lived in England in the 1750s; by the 1830s it was 13 million).

This phase also witnessed a transport revolution. Better roads were built, and so larger loads could be moved by horse-drawn wagons.

Transport became even more efficient with the cutting of canals, and by the 1820s England's major manufacturing towns were all joined to the canal network. Raw materials and finished goods could now be moved in greater quantities and over longer distances. However, by the 1830s the heyday of canals was over as a new form of transport – the railway – replaced them, marking the start of the second phase of the Industrial Revolution.

Beasts of burden

This is how much could be carried by horse, wagon and canal barge in the early 1800s.

- Packhorse   1/8 ton (0.127 tonne)
- Wagon, soft road   5/8 ton (0.635 tonne)
- Wagon, hard road   2 tons (2.03 tonnes)
- Barge, on river   30 tons (30.5 tonnes)
- Barge, on canal   50 tons (50.8 tonnes)

Here comes the train!

On 27 September 1825, a large crowd lined the route from Stockton to Darlington in northeast England, to catch a glimpse of a revolution in transport: the first steam-powered public railway in the world. The line may only have been 26 miles (40 km) long, but it was a sign of things to come, and within a few years the railway network had eclipsed canals and transformed the countryside, connecting cities, towns and villages. Transport times were cut and greater loads were moved than ever before.

Railway mania

This table shows the number of miles of track built in Britain during the first 40 years of the railway age (1 mile = 1.61 km). The peak years were the 1840s and 1850s, which gave rise to the term 'railway mania'.

Year	Miles of track in use
1830	98
1832	166
1834	298
1836	403
1838	743
1840	1,498
1842	1,939
1844	2,148
1846	3,036
1848	4,982
1850	6,084
1852	6,628
1854	7,157
1856	7,650
1858	8,354
1860	9,069
1862	9,953
1864	10,995
1866	11,945
1869	13,170
1871	13,388

It's faster by train

The Liverpool and Manchester Railway opened in 1830, linking the two towns with a 35-mile (56-km) railway line. It was the world's first passenger-carrying railway and it had a great effect on the existing road and canal links between the towns, as these figures from 1832 show:

	Canal	Coach	Rail
Passengers per day	0	688	1,070
Journey time (hours)	20	4	1¾

The first railway fatality

- **Who?** The Rt. Hon. William Huskisson, MP

- **When?** 15 September 1830

- **What happened?** He was a guest at the opening of the Liverpool and Manchester Railway and fell onto the track as a train approached. He was run over by Stephenson's *Rocket* and his leg was crushed; he died a few hours later.

The railway builders

Railways needed investors to provide the money, engineers to work out the routes and tens of thousands of men with picks, shovels and strong muscles to do the hard, back-breaking work of digging, levelling, blasting, tunnelling, bridging and tracklaying. These were the 'navigators', or 'navvies' for short, a tough breed of men who had honed their skills in the digging of canals. In the boom years of the 1840s, some 200,000 navvies were working to build the railway network.

Navvies' names

The Victorian railway network was built by the likes of Old Blackbird, Gorger, Hedgehog, Ginger Bill, Concertina Cockney and Jimmy-the-New-Man. These are nicknames, of course – the real names of these and just about every navvy were forgotten long, long ago.

The most famous of all navvy names belonged to three men in the 1840s who were known on railway construction sites all over England:

- **Wellington**: named after the Duke of Wellington, because he had a big nose.

- **Mary Ann**: named because of his effeminate voice.

- **Cat's Meat**: named after his previous job selling pet food. (There were some 300 pet-food dealers in London in the 1840s, selling horse meat from slaughterhouses to the capital's cat and dog owners)

Navvies worked in gangs which also attracted names – the Horseshoe Gang (named after an inn where they lodged), the Boys' Gang (men who were new to the job), and the Fly Away Gang, so named because they worked fast.

'Dens of wild men'

Navvies not only worked together, they lived together in shanties – crude, rough dwellings put up on land near to their places of work.

Some navvies lived on their own in small huts, others in groups of 20 or more in large buildings with bunks at one end and a kitchen at the other. Hundreds of men could be living in these shanty towns, the largest of which had their own shops where the men spent their weekly wages. They kept dogs for fighting or poaching, ate large amounts of bread, drank copious amounts of ale and got into fights.

Navvies lived as outcasts from the rest of society. They acquired a reputation for violence and alcoholism and were described as 'rude, rugged and uncultivated . . . possessed of great animal strength'. Another writer said their homes were 'dens of wild men'.

Navvy rhyming slang

bird lime	time
bo-peep	sleep
cherry ripe	pipe
china plate	mate
Dublin tricks	bricks
elephant's trunk	drunk
frog and toad	road
pig's ear	beer
Lord Lovell	shovel
Jimmy Skinner	dinner
Johnny Randle	candle
tiddlywink	drink

The growth of towns

As the railway network branched out across the nation, more people were able to travel than ever before. Towns such as Crewe in Cheshire and Swindon in Wiltshire rapidly swelled in size as they became railway headquarters. They were new towns for a new form of transport, and became known as 'railway towns'.

Crewe: Rail gateway to the north

In the 1830s the Grand Junction Railway Company chose the village of Crewe as the site for its locomotive works. The effect was dramatic:

Year	Population
1831	70
1841	203
1861	8,159
1871	17,810
1891	28,761

By 1851, for the first time in history, there were more people living in the towns of England than in the countryside.

Many people had continued the trend begun in the previous century: they'd moved to towns from rural villages and hamlets, leaving behind badly paid farmwork in search of better-paid factory jobs. It wasn't only the English who were on the move: thousands travelled south from Scotland, and even greater numbers came from Ireland following the famine that struck there in the 1840s. By the 1860s as many as 600,000 Irish were living in England.

Going to town

The population of some major industrial towns increased more than fourfold in just 50 years:

	1801	1851
Birmingham	71,000	233,000
Bristol	61,000	137,000
Leeds	53,000	172,000
Liverpool	82,000	376,000
Manchester	75,000	303,000
Sheffield	46,000	135,000

Jobs for the boys (and girls)

There were no health and safety laws for factories in the early 1800s. The working conditions were dangerous and both adults and children were forced to work long hours.

Boys and girls as young as 6 went out to work in England's coalmines and factories. Beatings were common, and so were accidents.

Chimney sweeps

Boys climbed inside chimneys to sweep away the soot caused by coal fires. A Nottingham master said this about his boys:

> The flesh must be hardened. This is done by rubbing it, chiefly on the elbows and knees, with the strongest brine, close by a hot fire. At first they will come back from their work with their arms and knees streaming with blood . . . then they must be rubbed with brine again.

How the other half lived

How Victorian children earned their keep

Samuel Coulson told a government enquiry in 1832 about the working conditions endured by his daughters in a Yorkshire mill:

What time did your girls start and finish work at the mill?
Start at 3 o'clock in the morning and finish at 10 o'clock at night.

What breaks did they get during their 19 hours of labour?
Breakfast a quarter of an hour, and dinner half an hour, and drinking water a quarter of an hour.

Had any of them any accident in consequence of this labour?
Yes, my eldest daughter . . . the cog caught her forefinger nail and screwed it off below the knuckle, and she was five weeks in Leeds Infirmary.

Has she lost that finger?
It is cut off at the second joint.

Have any of your children been strapped [beaten with a leather strap]?
Yes, every one.

Had your children any opportunity of sitting during those long hours of labour?
No.

The factory system was industrial slavery on a large scale until, in the 1830s, the government began to reform it. The Factory Act became law in 1833, and only then did conditions for children in England's textile mills begin to improve. Children working in other industries had to wait longer.

Further Acts followed, but as late as the 1860s, 11,000 children were still working in the Staffordshire pottery industry. Inspectors found that they worked 'under conditions which undermine their health and constitution'.

factory Act, 1833

- No child under the age of 9 could be employed in a mill.

- Children aged 9 to 13 could not work more than 8 hours a day in a mill, of which 2 hours must be given to education.

- Children aged 13 to 18 could not work more than 12 hours a day in a mill.

- Children under 18 must not work in a mill at night.

farewell to old England

It wasn't only England's industrial towns – Manchester, Birmingham, Sheffield and many others – whose populations swelled in the first decades of Queen Victoria's reign. The country's ports also grew as more goods and raw materials were imported and exported from England. London was by far the largest port, but Hull and Liverpool became increasingly busy – not just for the moving of goods, but for the moving of people.

The port of Hull is located on the east coast, facing the North Sea. Ships arrived from Scandinavia and Europe crowded with migrants – people leaving their own countries in search of new lives in other places.

In the 1830s fewer than 1,000 migrants passed through Hull each year. As the century wore on, the numbers increased until some 2,000,000 European migrants had arrived there. Some settled in England, usually in the industrial towns, where they found jobs. But, for most migrants, Hull was a stepping stone on a longer journey. From Hull, they travelled by train to the port of Liverpool on the west coast, where they boarded ships that crossed the Atlantic Ocean, taking them to the USA, Canada and South America (a 35-day journey). Some went on longer journeys to Australia and New Zealand – a voyage that lasted between 10 and 17 weeks.

By 1851, Liverpool was the leading emigration port in Europe (Le Havre, in France, was the second). Alongside Irish, Russian, Polish and many other nationalities were tens of thousands of English men, women and children, who said farewell to the country of their birth as their ships steamed west. These figures are just for English emigrants sailing from Liverpool:

Year	To North America	To Australia/ New Zealand
1825	14,292	485
1830	55,461	1,242
1840	72,935	15,850
1849	260,817	32,091

The Song of an Emigrant

Far away! O far away,
Over the wide sea's bounding spray,
Many a league o'er the pelting foam,
We seek a country, we seek a home!
Farewell, England! our native land,
Lingering still on thy verdant strand,
We look our last on thy once-loved
   shore,
And vow in our hearts to return no
   more.

Far away! O far away!
Nothing invites us here to stay.
England, our mother, is hard as stone,
And shuts her ear to her children's
   moan,
And running on to destruction sure,
Pampers the rich, and grinds the poor!
Farewell, England! A last farewell!
We fly thy shores, but we wish thee
   well.

Far away! O far away!
We seek a world o'er the ocean spray.
Welcome, O land across the sea,
Where bread is plenty, and man is free;
Welcome, the woods and deserts drear,
And boundless fields of another sphere.
Our sails are set, and the breezes swell,
England, our country – Farewell!
   Farewell!

Charles MacKay, c.1850

Catch cholera and die

The growth of England's towns brought a new kind of problem: overcrowding. With that came life-threatening diseases, particularly cholera, tuberculosis and smallpox. There were several cholera epidemics between the 1830s and the 1860s: thousands died after drinking water contaminated with sewage. Victims knew if they'd caught cholera because they had some or all of these symptoms:

- **Diarrhoea**: sudden, explosive, uncontrollable

- **Vomiting**: violent spewing out of clear fluid

- **Odd colour**: skin turning bluish-grey due to extreme dehydration (loss of fluids)

- **Black eyes**: eyes sunk back into eye sockets, surrounding skin looking black

- **Heartbeat**: fast, with a rapid pulse

- **Cramp**: severe pain in the legs

- **Weight loss**: no need to go on a diet to lose weight – cholera took care of that!

Death by water

The Broad Street cholera outbreak

In the summer of 1854 there was a serious outbreak of cholera in Broad Street, in the Soho district of London.

The first case was identified on 31 August, and within three days 127 people had caught cholera and died. A week later the death toll had risen to 500, and by the end of the outbreak 616 people were dead.

At the time, it was assumed that cholera was an airborne disease caught by breathing a 'miasma' of bad air. A local doctor, John Snow, disagreed, arguing that cholera entered the body through the mouth, not the nose.

Snow was sure the Broad Street outbreak was linked to a nearby well, so he put the street's water pump out of action by removing its handle. The cases of cholera began to diminish.

Snow was right. It turned out that the street's water supply was contaminated with raw sewage leaking into the well. The sewage contained the deadly cholera bacteria.

Made in England

England's factories and workshops were at the centre of the Industrial Revolution. The textile industry was the first to feel the full effects of the changing times, and these figures show just how dramatic this was:

Year	Handloom workers	Factory workers
1810	184,000	100,000
1820	240,000	126,000
1830	240,000	185,000
1840	123,000	262,000
1850	43,000	331,000

It was a pattern repeated in the other manufacturing industries. As the number of factory workers went up and new ways of making things were found, production of goods increased and the nation became the 'workshop of the world'. To showcase the country's new-found prosperity, an exhibition was planned for London.

Battle of the elms

Called 'The Great Exhibition of the Works of Industry of All Nations', the big event was planned for the summer of 1851. Hyde Park, London, was chosen as the site, but there was a problem. A group of ten elm trees stood where the main hall was to be built, and an outcry arose when the builders announced that they were to be chopped down.

The exhibition was the brainchild of Prince Albert, Queen Victoria's husband, and a cartoon was published in a leading magazine with the caption: 'Albert! spare those trees. Mind where you fix your show.'

Some said the exhibition was a folly, that for all the technological changes, for all the so-called 'progress', the human condition had not improved. For them, the Hyde Park elm trees were more important than an exhibition that was only going to be there a mere six months.

In the end a compromise was reached, and three of the great, leafy elms were enclosed within the exhibition hall itself.

The Great Exhibition was opened on 1 May 1851 by Queen Victoria and Prince Albert. Exhibitors had come from all over the world to display their goods, but for the visitors who flocked to marvel at the displays it symbolised Britain's economic domination of the world.

The Great Exhibition at a glance

- **When?** 1 May – 15 October 1851.

- **Where?** Hyde Park, London, in a massive iron and glass building nicknamed the Crystal Palace.

- **How big?** The building was 1,848 ft (563 m) long by 408 ft (124 m) wide, covering an area six times that of St Paul's Cathedral, England's largest cathedral at the time.

- **How many exhibitors?** 17,000 from around the world.

- **How many exhibits?** 100,000, from railway engines and steam hammers to porcelain and jewellery.

- **How many visitors?** 6 million, who ate 2 million buns and drank 1 million bottles of water between them.

'Albertopolis'

The Great Exhibition was a huge success. From the profits it made, 87 acres (32 ha) of land were bought for the nation in South Kensington, London, which became home to several well-known buildings:

- **Victoria and Albert Museum**
- **Science Museum**
- **Royal Albert Hall.**

The idea for these grand designs came from Prince Albert, who was keen to see new educational establishments in the capital. He was so involved in the scheme that by the late 1850s the area was nicknamed 'Albertopolis' in celebration of his role in Victorian life.

Prince Albert didn't live to see the project completed. He died in 1861, in the presence of the Queen and five of their nine children. The diagnosis was typhoid – a disease caused by drinking polluted water or milk, or eating contaminated food. Like that other killer of the time, cholera, typhoid could be caught by anyone – rich, poor, working-class or royal.

Victoria's children

Queen Victoria and Prince Albert were married in 1840. They had nine children: four boys and five girls.

1. Victoria Adelaide Mary (1840–1901), Princess Royal

2. Albert Edward (1841–1910), who became King Edward VII in 1901

3. Alice Maud Mary (1843–1878)

4. Alfred Ernest Albert (1844–1900), Duke of Edinburgh and of Saxe-Coburg-Gotha

5. Helena Augusta Victoria (1846–1923)

6. Louise Caroline Alberta (1848–1939)

7. Arthur William Patrick (1850–1942), Duke of Connaught and Strathearn

8. Leopold George Duncan (1853–1884), Duke of Albany

9. Beatrice Mary Victoria (1857–1944)

Ten things you didn't know about Queen Victoria

1. At Queen Victoria's coronation in 1838, the Coronation Ring, which had mistakenly been made to fit her little finger, was forced on to her ring finger by the Archbishop of Canterbury. After the ceremony it took her two hours to get the ring off.

2. Queen Victoria kept a diary for 69 years, from the age of 13 until a week before her death. She underlined important words or phrases two or even three times, and used lots of exclamation marks!

3. Did Queen Victoria really say 'We are not amused'? Contrary to popular belief, the answer is probably 'no'. In fact, her diaries are filled with the exact opposite: 'We were very much amused.'

4. In 1842, Queen Victoria became the first British monarch to travel by railway. The Great Western Railway (GWR) built a special royal coach to convey her from the station at Slough, Berkshire (near Windsor Castle), to Paddington Station, London.

5. In 1853, during the birth of her son Leopold, Queen Victoria became the first British monarch to be given chloroform as an anaesthetic.

6 When Queen Victoria's husband, Prince Albert, died in 1861, she was so grief-stricken that she was unable to attend his funeral.

7. Her first language was German, but from the age of 3 she was taught English. In 1887, aged 68, she started to learn Hindi, because of her role as Empress of India. She became good at speaking and writing it.

8. Seven attempts were made to assassinate her, in 1840, 1842 (twice), 1849, 1850, 1872 and 1882. In the 1850 attempt she was hit with a walking cane, crushing her bonnet and bruising her face. Her attacker was transported for 7 years.

9. She celebrated her Diamond Jubilee (60 years as queen) in 1897. She was 78 years old and, because she walked with difficulty and was unable to climb the steps to St Paul's Cathedral, the thanksgiving service was held outside with the Queen remaining in her carriage.

10. On her death in 1901, at the age of 81, she was buried with Prince Albert's dressing-gown and a plaster cast of his hand, a lock of hair from her faithful servant John Brown, a photograph of Brown clasped in her hand, several of his letters and a ring belonging to his mother.

The age of the middle class

When the 18-year-old Victoria became queen in 1837, society was largely divided between the rich and powerful upper class and the poor working class. But, by the 1850s, the middle class was coming increasingly to the fore.

The members of the middle class came from all walks of life, from prosperous merchants, factory owners and manufacturers to shopkeepers, craftsmen and tradesmen. They were likely to own property and have money in the bank, and their success had come about because of the new opportunities brought by the Industrial Revolution.

They were determined to give themselves as many chances to succeed in life as possible. They found ways to improve themselves by moving from manual work into 'trade' (shopkeeping, for example), and from trade into the professions (the law, banking, and so on). They worked hard, sent their children to school and went to church on Sunday. The middle class rose to dominate Victorian society – this was their time.

Boom time for Britain

The 6 million visitors – many of them middle-class – who thronged to the Crystal Palace in the summer of 1851 saw the nation at its showy, brilliant best. Here was the greatest show on earth in the world's greatest capital city, where, by sheer hard work and determination, just about anything was thought to be possible.

It was a golden age. Britain was reaping the rewards of her booming industries and her ships were exporting raw materials, finished goods and machines around the world. Foreign trade was such an important part of the economy that in the 1850s between 20 and 25 per cent of all world trade was British.

And with those British goods went the British way of working and organising, and so began another chapter in the nation's history – the Age of Empire.

Queen Victoria
with three of her successors:
Edward VII, George V
and Edward VIII

CHAPTER THREE

THE AGE Of EMPIRE

A Victorian atlas brought wide-eyed stares to many an English face. Spread out on the map of the world was the British Empire, and every country and far-flung island over which Britain had control was coloured red or pink. At the empire's greatest extent, as much as a quarter of the world's land surface and a fifth of its population was claimed by Britain. It was the largest empire ever known and, as at least one part of it was always in daylight, it was indeed 'the Empire on which the sun never sets'.

Empire building

The process of building an empire had begun long before Victorian times. In the early 1600s, Tudor colonists established a foothold in North America, some Caribbean islands were settled, and trading posts were set up in India. This was Britain's First Empire.

Although the North American adventure ended in 1783 when Britain lost control of America (except Canada), new lands were soon gained on the other side of the world. In 1788, New South Wales became the first British colony in Australia, and around the same time Sierra Leone in West Africa was established as a home for freed slaves.

Other early gains came about as a result of the wars with France (which ended in 1815) in which Trinidad, Malta, Gibraltar and the Cape of Good Hope passed into British hands.

But it was during the reign of Queen Victoria that Britain's empire really expanded, especially from the 1880s onwards.

Expansion of the British Empire

Some of the territories added to the British Empire between 1802 and 1902:

1802	Ceylon (now Sri Lanka)
1814	Cape of Good Hope
1814	Malta
1824	Singapore
1833	Falkland Islands
1840	New Zealand
1843	Gambia
1843	Hong Kong
1843	Natal (now part of South Africa)
1852	Burma
1858	India
1874	Fiji
1878	Cyprus
1882	Egypt
1884	Papua
1888	Brunei
1889	Northern Rhodesia (now Zambia)
1889	Southern Rhodesia (now Zimbabwe)
1890	Zanzibar (now part of Tanzania)
1894	Uganda
1895	East Africa Protectorate (now Kenya)
1899	Sudan
1900	Nigeria
1902	Orange Free State } (now parts of
1902	Transvaal } South Africa)

The end of slavery in the British Empire

In the 1560s English merchants took slaves from West Africa to work in the sugar plantations of the Caribbean. This was the beginning of the Atlantic slave trade which saw Africans captured and exported to Britain's colonies in North America and the Caribbean, where they were put to work in the production of sugar, tobacco and rice – crops that earned huge revenues for the British government.

The first rumbles of an anti-slavery movement emerged towards the end of the 1700s when evangelical Christians began a campaign to bring slavery to an end. At first the campaign to abolish slavery in the British Empire met with stiff opposition, as the governments of the day argued that it was essential to Britain's economic prosperity.

In 1823 the Anti-Slavery Society was formed in London, and among its founding members were several influential politicians, notably

William Wilberforce and Thomas Clarkson. A campaign during the 1830 general election encouraged the government to discuss the abolition of slavery, and in 1833 Parliament passed the Slavery Abolition Act.

It came into force on 1 August 1834, and on that day slavery was abolished throughout most of the British Empire (it was not abolished in British India until 1860). The purposes of the Slavery Abolition Act were described as:

1 the abolition of slavery throughout the British colonies

2 promoting the industry of the manumitted [freed] slaves

3 compensating the persons hitherto entitled to the services of such slaves.

The second purpose was achieved by providing freed slaves with a period of apprenticeship. The third purpose was secured by handing out £20 million in compensation to slave owners.

Ten things you didn't know about the British Empire

1. The Colonial Office in London was set up to organise, supervise and manage the colonies of the British Empire. The same building is today home to the Foreign and Commonwealth Office.

2. Some colonies, such as Cyprus and the Falkland Islands, were called 'protectorates'. These were territories where local rulers were left in charge. In principle, the British respected the local rulers and were prepared to defend them from foreign or internal threats.

3. Some colonies, such as Canada, were given the status of 'dominions'. They had significant freedom to rule themselves without too much interference from Britain.

4. The British Empire brought an end to the transportation of criminals to penal colonies in Australia. The practice was stopped in 1853 because gold had been found there in 1851, and the government wanted settlers – not convicts – to move there and unearth it.

5. In November 1852, three ships sailed up the River Thames to London loaded with 7 tons of Australian gold – the first of many.

6. Queen Victoria was proclaimed Empress of India on 1 January 1877. She was still mourning the death of her husband, Prince Albert, 16 years earlier; otherwise she would have travelled to India for the ceremony. As it was, her portrait was placed above the throne on which she would have sat, and a dignitary took her place.

7. India had the largest population of all the British Empire countries: about 300 million in the Victorian period.

8. A network of telegraph cables laid under the sea linked Britain and its colonies. The cables made long-distance communication possible. As maps marked the routes in red, the name 'All Red Line' was coined for the cable network.

9. The government wanted all the parts of the empire to know about each other, so allowed journalists to use the cable lines for only a penny a word. This was the 'Empire Press Rate'. Some of Queen Victoria's subjects knew more about what was going on elsewhere in the British Empire than they did about their own country.

10. A census was carried out in 1901 to find out how many people lived in the British Empire. The total came to 398,401,404, but the real figure was higher because some colonies only counted men.

Overseas conflicts

During the 19th century the British Empire fought many wars across its vast territories, particularly in India, Afghanistan and southern Africa.

First Anglo-Ashanti War	1823–1831
First Anglo-Afghan War	1839–1842
First Anglo-Sikh War	1845–1846
Second Anglo-Sikh War	1848–1849
Indian Rebellion	1857
Second Anglo-Ashanti War	1863–1864
Third Anglo-Ashanti War	1873–1874
Second Anglo-Afghan War	1878–1880
Anglo-Zulu War	1879
First Anglo-Boer War	1880–1881
Mahdist War	1881–1899
Fourth Anglo-Ashanti War	1895–1896
Anglo-Zanzibar War	1896
Second Boer War	1899–1902

Anglo-Zanzibar War: The shortest war in history

Date:	27 August 1896
Location:	Island of Zanzibar, off the coast of east Africa
Duration:	About 45 minutes (9.00 – 9.45 a.m.)
Casualties:	About 500
Result:	Decisive British victory

The conflict arose following a dispute over who would become the next sultan of Zanzibar. Five British warships bombarded the would-be sultan's palace, forcing him to flee, which allowed the British to appoint the sultan of their choice.

Marines after seizing the Palace, with broken Zanzibari Gun.

British marines outside the sultan's palace

War with Russia

The 19th century also saw Britain at war outside the Empire. In March 1854, Britain, France and Turkey declared war on Russia. Their aim was to stop Russia from gaining control of Serbia, Bosnia and Bulgaria, and from occupying Constantinople (Istanbul) in Turkey. It was a power struggle over control of the eastern Mediterranean.

The war was fought on the Crimean peninsula of southern Russia. It was the first war witnessed by photographers and newspaper reporters, and for the first time ever the reality of war touched people in Britain as they read about it in the papers.

Writing in *The Times* on 12 October 1854, war reporter William Russell said:

> It is with feelings of surprise and anger that the public will learn that no sufficient preparations have been made for the care of the wounded. Not only are there not sufficient surgeons . . . no dressers and nurses . . . there is not even linen to make bandages.

The reports shocked the government into action. Sidney Herbert, the Secretary-at-War, asked nurse Florence Nightingale to take charge of the army's hospitals in Turkey. He wrote: 'There is but one person in England that I know of who would be capable of organising and superintending such a scheme.'

Nightingale was posted to the British army Barrack Hospital at Scutari, Istanbul, Turkey. As she walked the gloomy hospital corridors she carried a lamp to light her way. The injured soldiers nicknamed her 'the Lady with the Lamp'.

Florence Nightingale became a national heroine, but the Crimean War is also remembered for the Battle of Balaclava, in which a misunderstood order sent a cavalry regiment charging into Russian guns. Of the 673 soldiers who took part in the Charge of the Light Brigade, 272 died. The event was immortalised by Tennyson, the Poet Laureate, in one of the most famous poems in the English language.

The Charge of
the Light Brigade

Half a league, half a league,
   Half a league onward,
All in the valley of Death
   Rode the six hundred.
'Forward, the Light Brigade!
Charge for the guns' he said:
Into the valley of Death
   Rode the six hundred.

'Forward, the Light Brigade!'
Was there a man dismay'd?
Not tho' the soldiers knew
   Some one had blunder'd:
Theirs not to make reply,
Theirs not to reason why,
Theirs but to do and die:
Into the valley of Death
   Rode the six hundred.

Cannon to right of them,
Cannon to left of them,
Cannon in front of them
   Volley'd and thunder'd;
Storm'd at with shot and shell,
Boldly they rode and well,
Into the jaws of Death,
Into the mouth of Hell
   Rode the six hundred.

Flash'd all their sabres bare,
Flash'd as they turned in air
Sabring the gunners there,
Charging an army while
    All the world wonder'd:
Plunged in the battery-smoke
Right thro' the line they broke;
Cossack and Russian
Reel'd from the sabre-stroke
Shatter'd and sunder'd.
Then they rode back, but not
    Not the six hundred.

Cannon to right of them,
Cannon to left of them,
Cannon behind them
    Volley'd and thunder'd;
Storm'd at with shot and shell,
While horse and hero fell,
They that had fought so well
Came thro' the jaws of Death,
Back from the mouth of Hell,
All that was left of them,
    Left of six hundred.

When can their glory fade?
O the wild charge they made!
    All the world wonder'd.
Honour the charge they made!
Honour the Light Brigade,
    Noble six hundred!

Alfred, Lord Tennyson

Improving society

Florence Nightingale was one of Victorian Britain's great social reformers. After the Crimean War ended in 1856, her organisational skills were put to use back home in England, where she set about reforming the training of nurses and improving the way hospitals worked.

She was one of many pioneers who changed Victorian society. Here are just a few of her fellow reformers:

- **Dr Thomas Barnardo** was concerned about the plight of thousands of children living rough on the streets of London, and in 1870 he opened the first of many children's homes that still bear his name.

- **Seebohm Rowntree** made a detailed study of poverty in York in the 1890s, which changed the way people thought about the poor and what should be done to help them.

- **Charles Booth** undertook surveys which showed that 30.7% of the working population of London was living in poverty.

Society was changing fast, and as the century neared its end many of the horrors of the first decades were beginning to disappear into history. Children now went to school, not to work; strict rules were put in place to make factories safer places in which to work (the Factory Acts); and, as town sewers and water supplies were improved, the killer disease cholera became a thing of the past.

Cookery for the working classes

Cookery books gave working-class people simple, affordable recipes, such as this one from 1852.

How to make Toast Water

A medicinal drink for invalids

Toast a piece of bread thoroughly browned to its centre without being burnt, put it into a jug, pour boiling water upon it, cover over and allow it to stand and steep until it has cooled; it will then be fit to drink.

Victorian sport and leisure

As working conditions improved, many people found they had more leisure time than ever before, and it didn't take long for Victorian entrepreneurs to work out what to do with it. Among them was Thomas Cook.

On 5 July 1841, Cook organised a railway outing from Leicester to Loughborough for 540 passengers. It may only have been a distance of 12 miles (19 km), but this was the world's first railway excursion and it led to the age of mass trips by train. Ten years later, it was the train that took tens of thousands of visitors on day excursions to London's Hyde Park to marvel at the Great Exhibition.

As the rail network reached towns on the coast, seaside holidays became increasingly popular, and resorts such as Brighton, Eastbourne, Southend, Blackpool and Scarborough grew in size. Their fortunes improved still further when bank holidays were introduced in 1871, allowing the masses to enjoy day trips to the seaside.

How the other half lived

Where the working classes had their fun

Blackpool, on the Lancashire coast, became the people's playground of northwest England – a status it has not entirely lost.

- Its rise to fame began in 1846, when the Preston and Wyre Railway opened a branch line to the town.

- In 1851 Blackpool's population was just 1,664. By 1881 it had swelled to 14,229.

- The resort was popular with factory workers from Manchester, Liverpool, Oldham, Bolton and the other industrial towns of Lancashire and northern England generally.

- Blackpool boasted sandy beaches and many other tourist attractions. By the 1890s it was a booming resort with a promenade complete with three piers, fortune-tellers, public houses, trams (it still has them today), donkey rides, fish-and-chip shops and theatres. In 1894 the famous Blackpool Tower was opened, inspired by the Eiffel Tower in Paris.

football – the national game

Perhaps the greatest change in how Victorians used their leisure time came with the rise of organised sport. By the end of the 19th century mass spectator sports had become a part of everyday life, and none more so than football.

1848: The first rules of the game were drawn up at Cambridge University (the Cambridge Rules).

1862: Notts County became the world's first professional football club.

1863: The Football Association was founded.

1871: The FA Cup competition began, with the first final held in 1872 between Wanderers and Royal Engineers. Wanderers, from London, won 1–0.

1872: The world's first official international match was held, between England and Scotland. It ended in a 0–0 draw.

1888: The Football League was formed, with 12 clubs.

What Victorian footballers wore

- In the early days of football, tops were known as 'jerseys'. In the 1880s, they began to be called 'shirts'.

- At first the game was played by men from the upper-middle class and minor aristocracy. They could afford handmade shirts from their tailors in their club's colours.

- In England's first international in 1872, players wore white woollen shirts and caps.

- Until 1928, there were no numbers on shirts to identify individual players.

- Players wore long knickerbockers or full-length trousers, often with a belt or braces.

- In 1890 the Football League ruled that no two member teams could register similar colours, so as to avoid clashes.

- Boots were made of heavy leather, had hard toecaps, and came high above a player's ankles.

- The first shin pads were worn in 1874, made from a cut-down pair of cricket pads and worn over the stockings.

The passing of the Victorian era

In 1887 Queen Victoria celebrated her Golden Jubilee – 50 years as Queen. Ten years later, aged 78, she celebrated her Diamond Jubilee – the first time a British monarch had reigned for 60 years.

On Monday 20 June 1897 she wrote in her diary: 'How well I remember this day sixty years ago when I was called from my bed by dear Mama to receive the news of my accession.'

A grand procession was held in London on 22 June, in which 17 carriages made their way slowly to St Paul's Cathedral for a service of thanksgiving.

Kings, queens and officials from around the world attended banquets and receptions; 1,310 telegrams of congratulations were sent to the Queen, as were many gifts. The prime minister of Hyderabad in India sent her a tiger's skull with a clock on top of it. A Mrs

Kendall gave her a bamboo walking stick. The Queen gave out honours and medals, and Nottingham, Bradford and Hull were made into cities.

Queen Victoria spent the first Christmas of the 20th century at Osborne House, her home on the Isle of Wight. There were concerns about her health, and a few days into the new year she took a turn for the worse. She died at 6.30 p.m. on Tuesday 22 January 1901.

Victoria had reigned for 63 years 216 days – the longest reign of any British monarch up to now. Her death brought the Victorian era to an end, an era in which Britain had changed beyond all recognition. Now, as a new monarch, King Edward VII, ascended the throne, a new century lay ahead with even greater changes to come.

A suffragette on hunger strike is force-fed ~ votes for women were not achieved without sacrifice

CHAPTER four

INTO THE 20th CENTURY

With the new century came a new monarch: on Victoria's death at the beginning of 1901 the crown passed to her son, and Edward VII became King of the United Kingdom of Great Britain and Ireland, Emperor of India and King of the British Dominions. His reign of nine years (1901–1910) was marked by the signing of treaties with other European countries, earning him the nickname 'Edward the Peacemaker' – but the 20th century turned out to be anything but peaceful, either at home or overseas.

Rise up, women!

The early years of the 20th century saw the struggle for women's suffrage – the right for women to vote in national elections.

Since the 1860s campaigners had been trying to get the law changed. Little by little, other groups in society had been allowed to vote in elections, but women had not.

At first, demands to give women the vote were peaceful and campaigners were known respectfully as 'suffragists'. Then, in 1903, Emmeline Pankhurst and her daughters Sylvia and Christabel formed the Women's Social and Political Union, and very soon the peaceful protests gave way to noisy demonstrations, window-smashing, letterbox fires and attacks on politicians.

The *Daily Mail* newspaper of 10 January 1906 branded these militant women 'suffragettes'. The word was intended to belittle them, but it was soon adopted as the preferred name by the movement.

Prisons filled with women prepared to go to jail for the right to vote. Many imprisoned suffragettes went on hunger strike, and some were force-fed through clamped-open mouths or nasal tubes.

In 1914, World War I began. It was the turning point for the campaign. As fathers, husbands, brothers and sons marched off to war the suffragettes halted their direct action and for the next four years women made an invaluable contribution to the nation's war effort. They nursed the wounded and worked in factories, steel mills, dockyards and on the land.

After four years of war, the government could no longer resist the cry of 'Votes for Women'. And so, in February 1918, an act of parliament was passed giving women aged over 30 the right to vote in elections. As a result, 8.5 million women became entitled to vote in the general election of 1918.

It took until 1928 for the age limit to be reduced to 21, finally giving women parity with men.

What suffragettes did

9 March 1906: A woman banged on the door of the prime minister's residence, 10 Downing Street, London, and another rushed inside. A third woman jumped onto the prime minister's car and addressed the crowd. All were arrested and released without charge.

23 October 1906: Suffragettes disrupted Parliament. Ten were arrested and sent to prison for two months.

13 February 1907: A march by suffragettes on Parliament turned violent as the police tried to break it up. Arrests were made and many were given 14-day prison sentences.

21 June 1908: As many as 250,000 protesters rallied in Hyde Park, London. A resolution was agreed 'that this meeting calls upon the government to grant votes to women without delay'.

29 June 1909: Thirteen suffragettes, using small stones wrapped in brown paper, smashed government windows at the Privy Council, Treasury and Home Offices.

2 July 1909: While in prison, suffragette Marion Dunlop went on hunger strike for 91 hours before being released.

13 November 1909: Liberal cabinet minister Winston Churchill was attacked in London by a suffragette wielding a riding-switch. She was sent to prison for a month.

21 November 1911: Windows were smashed at many government offices in London.

26 November 1912: Mailboxes in London and other cities were set alight, destroying thousands of items of mail. The plan was to get the public, whose mail had been burned, to put pressure on the government into giving women the vote. But it backfired, and the suffragettes lost support from the public.

18 February 1913: Suffragettes planted a bomb at the home of Chancellor of the Exchequer Lloyd George, destroying rooms.

3 June 1913: Emily Wilding Davison ran in front of the King's horse at the Epsom Derby. She was trampled, and died five days later.

10 March 1914: Velázquez's *Rokeby Venus* at London's National Gallery was slashed with a meat cleaver.

23 May 1914: A glass case holding an Egyptian mummy was smashed at the British Museum.

16 July 1914: The last major meeting held by suffragettes before the outbreak of war.

The war to end all wars

An event on the streets of Sarajevo, Bosnia, in June 1914 led to the start of the first global war. The assassination of Archduke Franz Ferdinand – heir to the throne of the Austro-Hungarian empire – must have seemed remote to the people of Britain, but within six weeks the nations of Europe were at war.

Britain had pledged to help Belgium and France should either country be attacked by Germany. On 3 August German troops invaded Belgium, and the following day Britain declared war on Germany. So began Britain's part in the 'war to end all wars', the World War or the Great War (it didn't become known as World War I until 1939 when a second global conflict began).

The Commander-in-Chief of the British army was Field Marshal Douglas Haig. The Government asked for 100,000 volunteers to swell the size of Haig's forces, but got 750,000 in just one month. Many believed the war would be over by Christmas 1914, but it dragged on for four long years.

The war was mainly fought on the Western Front – a narrow zone that ran through Belgium and France, in which the German army engaged the armies to its west: France, Britain (and the countries of the British Empire) and, from 1917, the USA.

But, in an age of new fighting technology, World War I crossed the English Channel and Britain itself came under attack from the air for the first time in history.

Zeppelins: Death from above

A new weapon came into service in the German military in 1909: a type of airship designed by, and named after, Count Ferdinand von Zeppelin. The first Zeppelin bombing raid against England came on 19 January 1915, when two Zeppelins attacked the eastern coastal towns of Great Yarmouth and King's Lynn, killing four civilians. Seven people were killed in the first Zeppelin attack on London on 31 May (16 Alkham Road, Stoke Newington, sustained London's first ever aerial bomb damage) and, on the night of 13–14 October 1915, five Zeppelins accounted for the lives of 71 Londoners.

Zeppelin attacks on England

How many raids?	208
How many bombs dropped?	5,907
How many killed?	556
How many injured?	1,914

Shot down in flames

On the night of 2–3 September 1916, over Cuffley, Hertfordshire, Lieutenant William Leefe Robinson, flying a converted B.E.2c night fighter, shot down the German airship SL 11. Flying at 11,500 ft (3,500 m), he raked the airship with specially developed incendiary ammunition, causing it to burst into flames.

This was the first time an enemy airship had been shot down, and for his action Robinson was awarded the Victoria Cross medal.

Long-range bombers

It wasn't only Zeppelins that brought death and destruction from above. From early in the war the first German bomber aircraft unleashed their load onto English towns.

The port of Dover, on the southeast coast, was the first to be bombed, in December 1914, but it wasn't until 1916 that German long-range bombers really started to make an impact, becoming the air weapon of choice as Zeppelins went out of favour.

The Germans created a bomber squadron for bombing England, named the 'England Squadron'. London, Dover, Folkestone, Chatham and Sheerness were all targeted.

Aircraft attacks on England

How many killed?	857
How many injured?	2,908

Attacked from the sea

It wasn't only air warfare that threatened England in World War I. Towns along the east coast came under attack from German battleships in the North Sea. Here are three examples of the German naval bombardment of England:

Date:	3 November 1914
Location:	Great Yarmouth
Casualties:	21 killed
	3 wounded

Date:	16 December 1914
Location:	Scarborough, Whitby and Hartlepool
Casualties:	137 killed
	592 wounded

Date:	24 April 1916
Location:	Great Yarmouth and Lowestoft
Casualties:	25 killed
	19 wounded

A *lost* generation

After the heavy naval bombardment of Scarborough in 1914, the message went out to 'avenge Scarborough', and thousands of young men enlisted in the armed forces.

By the time war ended on 11 November 1918, a generation had been lost. The final number of British casualties was massive:

Killed:	658,700
Wounded:	2,032,150
Missing:	359,150

Unknown warrior

On 11 November 1920, two years after the end of World War I, a coffin containing the body of an unidentified British soldier who had fallen on the Western Front was interred in Westminster Abbey, London. The coffin was buried in battlefield soil, in tribute to the missing who had died without trace during the conflict.

Ten things you didn't know about World War I

1. The 1914–1918 conflict is the sixth-deadliest war in world history. The total number of fatalities is unknown, but estimates range all the way from 15 to 65 million.

2. Trench warfare came to symbolise the war. By 1918, when the war ended, each side had dug at least 12,000 miles (19,000 km) of trenches, stretching from Belgium to Switzerland.

3. In cold, wet trenches, soldiers contracted 'trench foot' – a condition in which their feet went numb, became swollen and turned red or blue. In the worst cases, gangrene set in. During the winter of 1914–1915, the British army treated 20,000 soldiers for trench foot.

4. One third of all casualties on the Western Front are thought to have been killed or wounded in a trench.

5. France was the first country to use gas against enemy troops (teargas, which caused crying, sneezing and coughing). Germany was first to use poisonous chlorine gas. Soldiers were told to hold a urine-soaked cloth over their faces in a gas attack.

6. On Christmas Eve 1914, soldiers on both sides of the Western Front sang carols to each other. On Christmas Day, troops declared an unofficial truce along much of the Front. A year later, sentries on both sides were ordered to shoot anyone who attempted a repeat performance.

7. English nurse Edith Cavell was executed by a German firing squad in 1915. She had been arrested for helping Allied soldiers escape from German-occupied Belgium.

8. The greatest single loss of life in the history of the British Army occurred during the Battle of the Somme on 1 July 1916, when 50,000 soldiers were killed, injured or declared missing on the first day of the battle.

9. It is estimated that over 800,000 warhorses were killed in the line of duty while serving with the British Army on the Western Front.

10. Henry Tandey, VC, DCM, MM was the most highly decorated British private of the war. According to a (probably invented) story, he decided not to shoot a wounded German soldier whom he saw after the Battle of Marcoing in 1914. 'I took aim but couldn't shoot a wounded man,' Tandey is supposed to have said, 'so I let him go.' Years later he discovered that he had spared a German corporal named Adolf Hitler.

The forgotten fallen

Barely had the guns of World War I been silenced when a different kind of killer struck.

In the spring of 1918, a deadly strain of the influenza ('flu') virus spread around the world. Because Spanish newspapers were the first to write about the virus in any detail, it acquired the name 'Spanish flu', though it did not start there.

No-one knows where the virus first appeared – British Army camps along the Western Front, US Army training camps and New York City have all been suggested. One thing, though, is clear: infected troops who returned home after the war passed the virus on to family, friends and strangers.

Spanish flu reached Britain in May 1918. The first cases were recorded in Scotland, and within weeks no part of Britain was safe. At first, doctors said it was a 'three-day fever', but as patients died in growing numbers, the true scale of the epidemic was realised.

School's closed!

Schools were closed in an attempt to stop the spread of the virus. Children, who were warned about the risk of infection, came up with this playground rhyme:

> I had a little bird,
> Its name was Enza;
> I opened the window
> And in flew Enza.

In towns across England, streets were sprayed with chemicals and people wore anti-germ masks. The *News of the World* newspaper suggested ways to combat the epidemic:

> Wash inside nose with soap and water each night and morning; force yourself to sneeze night and morning, then breathe deeply. Do not wear a muffler; take sharp walks regularly and walk home from work; eat plenty of porridge.

By the time the epidemic ended in 1919, the death toll in Britain was 228,000 – the worst epidemic to have affected the nation since the Black Death of 1348.

119

When the boys came home

At the end of World War I, in November 1918, the British army numbered 3.8 million men. With the war over, soldiers were demobilised – released from service – and returned to their prewar civilian lives.

Year	Army personnel
1918	3,800,000
1919	900,000
1922	230,000

Britain had emerged on the winning side in World War I, and Prime Minister David Lloyd George was hailed as 'the man who won the war'. He called a general election for December 1918 (the first election in which women were allowed to vote), and during a campaign speech he promised to make Britain 'a land fit for heroes'. This slogan helped to win him a landslide victory.

David Lloyd George
(1863–1945)

The troubled twenties

In 1918, Britain still depended on the industries that had made the nation successful in the 19th century: iron, steel, textiles, coal and shipping. But World War I had changed everything, and postwar Britain was a very different place.

Countries that Britain had once exported to had now set up their own manufacturing industries and no longer needed to buy British goods. For example, before the war India had taken 13 per cent of all British exports, especially textiles. After the war, India established its own textile mills and during the 1920s bought less and less finished cloth from Britain. The war did more harm to Britain's textile industry than to any other, and the Lancashire cotton industry went into a steep decline from which it never recovered.

It was a pattern repeated in other industries across Britain, and very soon the notion of 'a land fit for heroes' was little more than a political dream.

Slump and strike

Before the war, unemployment in Britain had been between 5 and 10 per cent of the working population. The war years saw industries at full stretch, and unemployment fell.

The boom time continued for about two years after the war, but from the summer of 1920 industries slowed down, the export of goods fell and unemployment returned. It was the start of a time of depression around the world.

For Britain, the industry which suffered most was coal. In the years before the war Britain's mines had supplied 10 per cent of the world's coal, but after the war, as foreign pits became more productive, demand for British coal fell; by 1925 the export figure was 7 per cent.

Demand for coal at home also fell. Ships, including those of the Royal Navy, switched from coal to oil; power stations became more efficient, burning less coal to make more electricity; and householders cut back on what they used. With less demand for coal, the industry shrank and workers were laid off.

Unemployment in Britain doubled between 1920 and 1938:

Year	Unemployed
1920	900,000
1921	1,200,000
1922	1,900,000
1923	1,500,000
1924	1,300,000
1925	1,200,000
1926	1,400,000
1927	1,100,000
1928	1,200,000
1929	1,200,000
1930	1,900,000
1931	2,700,000
1932	2,700,000
1933	2,500,000
1934	2,200,000
1935	2,000,000
1936	1,800,000
1937	1,500,000
1938	1,800,000

'Not a penny off the pay, not a second on the day'

As coalminers swelled the ranks of the unemployed, those who kept their jobs faced the threat of pay cuts and longer working hours. Mine owners wanted to reduce wages by 13 per cent and increase shifts from 7 to 8 hours a day. The miners demanded 'Not a penny off the pay, not a second on the day,' and called on the trade union movement for support.

The 1926 General Strike

When negotiations between miners and mine owners broke down, it was inevitable that strike action would happen, and, for 9 days in May 1926, there was a General Strike.

30 April: The mine owners acted first by locking miners out of their pits.

4 May: A general strike was called by the Trades Union Congress (TUC) to support the miners. More than 2 million members of the transport, rail, docks, printing, gas and electricity, building, iron, steel, chemical and coal unions came out on strike.

5–6 May: The government was prepared and acted fast. It sent in soldiers and volunteers to unload cargoes at docks, drive buses and trains, and distribute food.

7 May: Police and strikers clashed in Liverpool, Hull and London. The government seized paper supplies so the TUC's newspaper *The British Worker* could not be printed.

8 May: Police made baton-charges on rioting strikers in Glasgow, Hull, Middlesbrough, Newcastle and Preston.

10 May: Textile workers joined the strike. Prime Minister Stanley Baldwin declared that Britain was 'threatened with a revolution'.

12 May: The TUC called off the strike. The strikers were taken by surprise and drifted back to work, except for the miners. They stayed on strike until November, when they were forced back to work on the mine owners' terms: less pay, longer hours.

Society divided

The General Strike ended in failure for the trade unions and the workers they represented. The unions lost members, and the strike highlighted divisions in British society. The working class had gone out on strike, but the middle class had come forward as volunteers to break the strike and keep the nation's essential services functioning.

For the middle class, the General Strike was not about workers' pay and conditions, but about who should run the country. The strike came a few years after the Russian Revolution of 1917, in which working-class Russians had overthrown their leaders and taken control of the country. There was a real fear amongst many people that a similar revolution could happen in Britain, and this was why the government had refused to give in to the strikers and why so many fellow Britons had refused to support them.

How the other half lived

How the rich got by in the Roaring Twenties

Not everyone felt the pinch in the 1920s. The rich enjoyed a heady lifestyle of parties, glitzy social events, and an increasing use of cars and telephones – luxuries that were out of reach for most of the population.

The very rich, who lived in country houses or grand town houses, might still employ some or all of these servants and helpers:

- **Butler:** head servant
- **Housekeeper:** keeps the house in good order
- **Cook:** in charge of the kitchen
- **Footman:** the butler's assistant
- **Housemaid:** cleans the house, serves meals
- **Lady's maid:** attends the mistress of the house
- **Valet:** attends the master of the house
- **Kitchen maid:** prepares food, washes up, and does other menial tasks
- **Governess:** private teacher who lives in and teaches the family's children
- **Nanny:** looks after the youngest children and the nursery
- **Nurserymaid:** attends the children
- **Gardener:** tends the garden and grounds
- **Coachman:** in charge of horse-drawn carriages
- **Groom:** in charge of horses
- **Chauffeur:** driver in charge of the motor car.

The Great Depression

On Thursday 24 October 1929, the US stock market crashed as traders panicked and sold millions of shares at rock-bottom prices. It triggered a worldwide economic crisis, known as the Great Depression, that affected Britain and lasted for most of the 1930s.

How hard was life during the Depression?

Although unemployment in Britain went up during the Depression and food handouts became a way of life for many, life was not hard for everyone.

As prices fell, those who had money bought luxury goods such as vacuum cleaners, washing machines, radios and the first TVs. There was a housing boom (3 million new houses were built in the 1930s), free milk was given to schoolchildren, and many had more leisure time for holidays, and for going to the cinema, dance halls, swimming baths and sporting events.

Hunger marches

Apart from strikes, unemployment and low wages brought another form of protest onto Britain's streets in the 1920s and 1930s. Several so-called 'hunger marches' were staged (the first was in 1922), in which men and women marched from around the country to protest outside Parliament in London. Their purpose was to draw attention to the plight of the unemployed who, without money to buy food, faced hunger.

National Hunger March, 1932

On 27 October 1932, 3,000 marchers arrived in London with a petition containing a million signatures, and joined a crowd of 100,000 at Hyde Park. The protest ended in violence when the crowd was dispersed by mounted police, who confiscated the petition before it could be delivered to the government.

The Jarrow March, 1936

In October 1936, 207 men marched from Jarrow, near Newcastle-upon-Tyne, to London. Their once-thriving community of steel and ship workers had been blighted by lack of work: 7 out of every 10 workers were unemployed.

The Jarrow March – or Jarrow Crusade as it was also known – was not the largest of the hunger marches, but it was the one that had the most impact.

Marching in stages of 15–20 miles (24–32 km) a day, the men covered the 300 miles (480 km) in 22 days. Wherever the marchers stopped for the night, local people gave them food and shelter.

Their arrival in London was an anticlimax. A petition of 11,000 signatures was presented to Parliament, but Prime Minister Stanley Baldwin refused to meet the marchers, saying he was 'too busy'.

The marchers were given £1 each for the train fare home from London. Jarrow's shipbuilding industry remained closed.

The year of three kings

1936 was a difficult year for the British monarchy. One king died, one was never crowned, and one never thought he'd be king.

King George V

The king who died was George V. His long reign had seen Europe torn apart by war, and in 1917, with anti-German feeling running high, he had changed the royal family's surname from the Germanic Saxe-Coburg-Gotha to Windsor, which sounded reassuringly English.

George V had seen the British Empire reach its greatest extent in the early 1920s, and the British Empire Exhibition of 1924–1925 had set out to bring the 58 countries of the Empire closer to the 'mother country'.

But the signs of an empire on the verge of breaking up were already there. Ireland had gained independence from Britain in 1922; only the six northern counties (Northern Ireland) remained part of the United Kingdom.

George V's 1935 Silver Jubilee – 25 years as monarch – was a time to celebrate, but his death in January 1936 led to a crisis.

King Edward VIII

George V was succeeded by his eldest son, David (as he was usually called), who took his first name, Edward, as his official name.

King Edward VIII was aware of the hardship which the Great Depression was causing for millions, and in the summer of 1936 he showed his support for the unemployed by saying that 'Something must be done to find these people work.' This was not well received by the government – and neither was his relationship with a divorced American woman, Mrs Wallis Simpson.

The government gave Edward a choice – marry Mrs Simpson and abdicate (give up the crown), or end his relationship with Mrs Simpson and remain king. He chose love over duty, and in December 1936 he abdicated. As he had not had a coronation ceremony, Edward VIII was 'Britain's uncrowned king'.

King George VI

Next in line to the throne was George V's younger son, Albert. Like his brother David, he too picked another of his names for his official title, and on 12 May 1937 – the date planned for Edward VIII's coronation – he was crowned King George VI.

George VI had expected to enjoy a reasonably quiet family life as the Duke of York; but, with kingship unexpectedly thrust upon him, everything changed.

When George VI became king, Britain was starting to come out of the Great Depression. Unemployment was still over the one million mark, but it was falling as the threat of a new war with Germany loomed closer and Britain's factories stepped up production of essential goods.

The Battle of Britain:
'so much owed by so many
to so few'

CHAPTER FIVE

WORN OUT BY WAR

Standing on the tarmac of Heston Aerodrome, London, Prime Minister Neville Chamberlain held a piece of paper aloft for all to see. It was 30 September 1938, and Chamberlain had just flown in from Munich, Germany, where he'd thrashed out an agreement with the German chancellor, Adolf Hitler. The Munich Agreement was, he said, 'symbolic of the desire of our two peoples never to go to war with one another again'. Later that day, outside 10 Downing Street, he said, 'I believe it is peace for our time.' How wrong he was.

'This country is at war with Germany'

In March 1939, just 6 months after the Munich Agreement was signed, the German army seized Czechoslovakia. In doing this, Adolf Hitler broke the Munich Agreement and Prime Minister Chamberlain realised that it was not worth the famous piece of paper it was written on. Some people had been telling him that all along, including one of his own politicians, the MP for Epping, Winston Churchill. Chamberlain's 'peace for our time' was looking increasingly fragile.

World War II began at dawn on 1 September 1939, when one million German troops crossed into Poland and some 1,500 warplanes went into action.

Two days later, at 11.15 a.m. on 3 September, Prime Minister Chamberlain addressed the nation. People stopped what they were doing and gathered around wireless sets to hear his solemn words.

This is what they heard:

This morning the British Ambassador in Berlin handed the German Government a final Note stating that, unless we heard from them by 11 o'clock that they were prepared at once to withdraw their troops from Poland, a state of war would exist between us.

I have to tell you now that no such undertaking has been received, and that consequently this country is at war with Germany.

Conscription

When war broke out the British Army could muster only 897,000 men. More were urgently needed, so the National Service (Armed Forces) Act made all able-bodied men between 18 and 41 liable for conscription.

By the end of 1939 more than 1.5 million men had been conscripted ('called up') to join the British armed forces. Of those, just over 1.1 million went to the army and the rest were shared between the Royal Navy and the Royal Air Force.

Germany prepares to invade

After Germany's defeat of France in spring 1940, Hitler believed that Britain would surrender. As that didn't happen, on 16 July 1940 Hitler issued Führer Directive No. 16. Its title was: *On Preparations for a Landing Operation against England*.

Not since 1066 had a foreign army invaded England (apart from William III's invasion-by-invitation of 1688 – see Vol. 2, page 109). The Spanish had tried and failed in 1588, and Napoleon had thought about it in 1803–1805. Now, in the words of Hitler's Directive:

> Since England, in spite of her hopeless military situation, shows no signs of being ready to come to an understanding, I have decided to prepare a landing operation against England and, if necessary, to carry it out.

> The aim of this operation will be to eliminate the English homeland as a base for the prosecution of the war against Germany and, if necessary, to occupy it completely.

The invasion codename was Operation Sea Lion.

Operation Sea Lion

- The target date for the German invasion of England was 15 August 1940.

- The invasion force would be made up of 260,000 troops, 62,000 horses and 34,000 vehicles.

- The Luftwaffe (German Air Force) was moved to airfields in northern France. The Germans claimed they would smash the air defences of southern England in 4 days, and wipe out the RAF in 4 weeks.

- With the south coast air defences destroyed, the German plan was to land 90,000 troops and capture key ports in Kent and Sussex. The bulk of the German army would then come ashore and march on London.

- A wanted list of 2,300 leading people was compiled – they were to be rounded up and detained immediately.

- When the RAF showed no sign of being wiped out, the invasion date was moved back to 27 September, then to 8 October and finally to spring 1941 – by which time Hitler had turned his attention to the Eastern Front, and Operation Sea Lion was called off.

Sky-high heroes

On 20 August 1940, Prime Minister Winston Churchill (who had succeeded Neville Chamberlain in May) gave one of his most famous wartime speeches. He was reviewing the progress of the war to a packed House of Commons, and one sentence in particular has gone down in history:

> Never in the field of human conflict was so much owed by so many to so few.

At this point a great cheer went up from the House. Churchill was paying tribute to the heroism of the pilots of the Royal Air Force (RAF), whose actions over the skies of southern England in the summer of 1940 had thwarted German plans to invade England.

In an earlier speech, on 18 June 1940, Churchill had said:

> The Battle of France is over. The Battle of Britain is about to begin.

The Battle of Britain

As Churchill had predicted, the air battle of summer 1940 – the Battle of Britain – was Britain's critical battle for survival. Defeat was not an option.

- It's estimated that between July and October 1940 the RAF lost around 1,023 aircraft whilst the Luftwaffe lost 1,887.

- The average age of an RAF pilot was 22.

- The Luftwaffe's main fighter planes were the Messerschmitt Bf 109 and Bf 110. Its bomber planes included the Dornier Do 17, the Junkers Ju 88, the Heinkel He 111 and the Junkers Ju 87 (also known as the 'Stuka', from *Sturzkampfflugzeug*, the German word for 'dive bomber').

- The main fighter planes of the RAF were the Hawker Hurricane and the Supermarine Spitfire.

- In the opening stages of the battle, German bombers targeted military airfields. Tactics were later changed, and from September 1940 London became the primary target – and the Blitz began.

London's burning!

The English called the German bombing campaign against London and other cities the Blitz (from the German word for 'lightning'). The Blitz began in the summer of 1940, as the daylight Battle of Britain was nearing its end. With no signs of the RAF weakening, Hitler issued orders on 5 September 'for disruptive attacks on the population and air defences of major British cities, including London, by day and night'.

The aim was to inflict terror and exhaustion on the British population in the hope that morale would collapse. The London Blitz began on 7 September, when 300 bombers attacked in the daytime and 180 at night. The raids claimed the lives of 430 Londoners and marked the start of 76 consecutive nights of bombing (apart from the night of 3 November, when it was too cloudy). By May 1941, when the worst of the campaign was over, more than 25,000 tons (25,400 tonnes) of bombs had fallen onto British towns and cities, killing some 43,000 civilians and injuring 139,000.

The bombing of Coventry

- **When was it?** During the night of 14–15 November 1940.

- **How many bombers?** 509 German bombers set out from bases in France; 449 reached Coventry, an industrial city in the English Midlands. The German codename for the raid was *Mondscheinsonate* ('Moonlight Sonata').

- **How long did the raid last?** 12 hours.

- **What was the damage?** Three quarters of Coventry's factories destroyed (including 12 armaments factories); the historic city centre almost completely destroyed, including the magnificent 14th-century cathedral; 4,330 homes destroyed.

- **What were the casualties?** About 554 people killed and 865 injured.

- **And the Germans said what?** The raid gave the German language a new word for 'totally destroyed': *c o v e n t r i e r t* ('Coventried').

Wartime food

Food was in short supply, and the Ministry of Food issued leaflets with economical recipe ideas. One was called *How to Use Stale Crusts*. It now became illegal to feed bread to wild birds – all bread was to be used to feed people.

Woolton pie

This famous recipe, created by the head chef at the Savoy Hotel, London, was named after Frederick Marquis, 1st Earl of Woolton, who became Minister of Food in 1940.

- 1lb each of diced potatoes, cauliflower, carrots, swede
- 3 or 4 spring onions
- 1 tablespoon oatmeal
- 1 teaspoon vegetable extract

Cook all together for 10 minutes with water to cover. Stir to prevent sticking. Allow to cool. Put into a pie dish. Sprinkle with chopped parsley. Cover with a crust of potato or wheatmeal pastry. Bake until browned. Serve hot with brown gravy.

Rationing

Food rationing started on 8 January 1940. Ration quantities varied throughout the war depending on what was available, but a typical week's ration for one adult was:

- Bacon and ham: 4 oz (100 g)
- Meat: 1 shilling's worth (about £3 today)
- Butter: 2 oz (50 g)
- Cheese: 2 oz (50 g)
- Margarine: 4 oz (100 g)
- Cooking lard: 2 oz (50 g)
- Milk: 3 pints (1800 ml)
- Tea: 2 oz (50 g)
- Sugar: 8 oz (225 g)
- Eggs: 1

These food items were also rationed:

- Dried milk: 1 packet every 4 weeks
- Dried eggs: 1 packet every 4 weeks
- Sweets: 12 oz (350 g) every 4 weeks
- Preserves and jams: 1 lb (450 g) every 4 weeks

Ten things you didn't know about World War II

1. Villages in England were taken over by the Ministry of Defence. The populations of Imber, on Salisbury Plain, Wiltshire, and Tyneham, Dorset, were evacuated. Both villages were used for training purposes. Today, they are ghost villages.

2. Some 827,000 schoolchildren (and their teachers) were evacuated from towns and cities to safer places far away from where German bombs were expected to fall.

3. Metal railings were ripped up from streets and properties around the country so they could be melted down to make weapons and other war items. In fact, most ended up being thrown away.

4. King George VI and Queen Elizabeth remained in Buckingham Palace, their London home, for most of the war. It was hit nine times by German bombs. Their daughters, Princess Elizabeth and Princess Margaret Rose, were evacuated to Windsor Castle in Berkshire.

5. The government encouraged people to eat carrots. 'Carrots help you see in the dark' was a popular saying, and was widely believed.

6. The nightly blackout plunged towns and cities into darkness, making it hard for German bombers to spot them. Car headlights were covered so that only a tiny slit of light shone out. Car bumpers, bicycle mudguards, kerbstones and tree trunks were painted white.

7. Charity Bick, from West Bromwich, was awarded the George Medal for bravery in dealing with incendiary bombs as they fell on buildings. At 16, she was the youngest recipient of this medal during the war.

8. People were told not to use more than 5 inches (13 cm) of water in their baths. Less bathwater meant that less coal was needed to heat it. Coal was needed in factories making supplies for the war.

9. On 13 June 1944, the first V-1 flying bomb struck London. Also known as a 'buzz bomb' or 'doodlebug', 10,000 were launched against England. Many were shot down, but 3,531 fell on England – 2,419 of these on London. The V-2 rocket was bigger, and 1,054 fell on England – 517 on London.

10. The Crown Jewels were removed from the Tower of London and hidden at a secret location. Over the years, rumours have spread saying they were stored at a Cheshire salt mine, sent to Canada, or even locked inside Fort Knox, USA. In fact, they were probably safely stored at Windsor Castle.

Postwar Britain

On 7 May 1945, Germany surrendered and the war in Europe was over. The next day was declared VE (Victory in Europe) Day, and as Prime Minister Winston Churchill was driven to the House of Commons, he gave his famous 'V for victory' sign to the crowds celebrating on London's streets.

But, just 57 days later, Britain's wartime leader was defeated in a general election. It seemed hard to believe that the very people Churchill had worked to save in World War II now rejected him at the ballot box. It was – and still is – one of the biggest shocks in British political history.

One reason why Churchill lost the 1945 general election was that he had completed the task he had taken on in 1940, and in a way this made him redundant. The public saw him as their wartime leader, not their peacetime prime minister. For that, a different leader was needed, and Clement Attlee of the Labour Party won with a landslide victory.

The age of austerity

In the years after World War II, Britain was in a bad way. Towns and cities had to be rebuilt, the road and rail network had to get Britain moving again, and factories that had produced war goods now had to switch to other things.

Rebuilding Britain would require capital the government didn't have, added to which it owed money loaned by the USA. Britain was broke, penniless, and needed to earn money. The way to do that was by exporting goods.

Until Britain could pay its way in the world as it had before the war, the nation endured years of hardship. Rationing of food and clothing continued, and in 1946 the Ministry of Food even circulated a recipe for squirrel pie! The bitterly cold winter of 1946–1947 didn't help, either. Coal stocks ran low and the lights went out as electricity supplies were cut.

In this age of austerity, Britain's wartime 'make do and mend' spirit carried on much as before.

'from cradle to grave'

Despite the hardships, the 1940s laid the building blocks of a new Britain, the cornerstone of which was the creation of the welfare state.

World War II had brought to a head the growing feeling that the state had a duty to protect its citizens 'from cradle to grave'.

In 1942 the Beveridge Report had identified 'five giant evils' which the state had to defeat if reforms to the welfare system were to work:

- **Want** (i.e. poverty): to be ended by National Insurance

- **Disease:** to be ended by a National Health Service

- **Ignorance:** to be ended by education

- **Squalor:** to be ended by slum clearance and new housing

- **Idleness** (unemployment): to be ended by jobs for all.

In 1945, Prime Minister Attlee announced that he would introduce the welfare state outlined in the Beveridge Report, and in 1948 the National Health Service (NHS) came into being, offering free medical treatment for all.

Britain's welfare state was created during the years of postwar austerity, which only added to the financial burdens on the already strained economy.

Nationalisation

The Labour government also brought in nationalisation, when a swathe of British industry was taken into public ownership.

The gas, water, coal, electricity, iron and steel industries, as well as the railways and road haulage industry, came under government control and effectively became public property. Labour was committed to public ownership as a way of helping these key industries which were run down and struggling because of the war.

from Empire to Commonwealth

The phrase 'Commonwealth of Nations' was coined in the 1880s to describe the countries of the British Empire. By 1945, Britain's capacity to govern them was weakened. As many of them achieved independence, the British Empire gradually evolved into an association of former British territories.

Things can only get better

Amid the political and social changes and the years of austerity, the postwar period did bring happier times for some.

In November 1947, Princess Elizabeth married Philip Mountbatten, Duke of Edinburgh. Among their wedding presents was a chicken from a girl in the USA, who sent it in the knowledge of Britain's food rationing. She asked for the wishbone to be sent back to her! The following year, Princess Elizabeth gave birth to a son, Charles.

London Olympics, 1948

London became host city of the 1948 Summer Olympics, an event that came to be known as the Austerity Games because of the postwar economic climate and rationing.

Because of their roles as aggressors in World War II, Germany and Japan were not invited to participate.

Great Britain finished in 12th place in the medal table with a tally of 23 medals: 3 gold, 14 silver, 6 bronze.

Birth of the Paralympics

To coincide with the start of the 1948 Olympics, neurologist Dr Ludwig Guttmann organised an archery contest at Stoke Mandeville Hospital in Buckinghamshire. The competitors were wheelchair-using war veterans with spinal injuries. This event was the forerunner of the modern Paralympic Games.

Dr Guttmann, who had come to Britain as a refugee from Nazi Germany, was knighted in 1966.

'A tonic to the nation'

As the 1950s dawned, life in Britain was gradually becoming easier. In May 1950, petrol rationing ended and motorists were once again able to enjoy the freedom of the road.

A year later, in May 1951, King George VI opened the Festival of Britain, held to mark the centenary of the Great Exhibition and to be a showcase of British goods and design.

The Festival director described it as 'a tonic to the nation', and that summer 8.5 million visitors went to the main site on London's South Bank, where modern, futuristic exhibition halls had been built on derelict, bomb-scarred land. At its centre was the Dome of Discovery – the world's largest dome at the time – housing displays about Earth and space.

The Festival of Britain was a very public sign of optimism that the hard times of austerity were over – or soon would be.

The King is dead, long live the Queen!

At the end of January 1952, Princess Elizabeth began a royal visit to Kenya. She had taken the place of her father, King George VI, who was too ill to make the trip.

On 6 February the king died peacefully in his sleep at Sandringham House, a royal residence in Norfolk.

Princess Elizabeth, who had flown out from Britain a princess, returned home as Queen Elizabeth II. She was just 25 years old. And so began the start of a long and eventful reign.

The swinging sixties:
after the austerity of the
postwar years, the outlook
finally began to seem brighter

CHAPTER SIX

THE NEW ELIZABETHAN ERA

ack in 1559, a 25-year-old queen was crowned at Westminster Abbey. Her name was Elizabeth – the first English queen of that name. Now, on Tuesday 2 June 1953, Westminster Abbey was again the setting for a coronation ceremony, and as the crown was placed on the head of another 25-year-old Elizabeth, no-one could have imagined that the reign of Queen Elizabeth II was going to span many decades ahead, making her one of the longest-reigning monarchs in history. A new Elizabethan era had begun.

'Never had it so good'

The year of Queen Elizabeth II's coronation, 1953, was notable for two achievements that offered excitement and hope for the future.

First, on Coronation Day itself, news came through that a team of mountaineers from Britain had become the first to reach the top of Mount Everest, the world's highest mountain.

Later that year, the Conservative government of Prime Minister Winston Churchill (he had been returned to power in 1951, though at 77 he was little more than a figurehead) announced that a record 300,000 new homes had been built that year.

Ordinary people began to fill their homes with electrical goods and luxury items. Housework was made easier by the vacuum cleaner, the washing machine, the electric iron and cooker. Many bought fridges and freezers for the first time, cosy carpets replaced hard linoleum, and mass-produced furniture, colourful fabrics and wallpapers became the height of 1950s fashion.

In this new age of plenty, one 'must have' item was at the top of many a family shopping list: a television set. It was the young queen herself who insisted her coronation be televised for all to see (the government didn't want to), and millions of people gathered around tiny televisions to watch the great ceremony in grainy black and white. Many had bought their first television just so they could watch the Coronation, and many more went out and bought one after the event.

In July 1957, Conservative prime minister Harold Macmillan gave a speech in which he remarked:

> You will see a state of prosperity such as we have never had in my lifetime – nor indeed in the history of this country. Indeed let us be frank about it – most of our people have never had it so good.

Macmillan was referring to the rise in living standards, near-full employment, higher wages, consumerism and the end of rationing.

Off the ration

Rationing was a legacy of World War II. It came to an end in stages, over a period of 6 years between 1948 and 1954. When government control of an item ended, it was said to be 'off the ration'.

July 1948: flour and bread – the first things to come off the ration

December 1948: jams and preserves

March 1949: clothes

January 1950: milk

May 1950: canned and dried fruit, chocolate biscuits, treacle, syrup, jellies and mincemeat

September 1950: soap

October 1952: tea

February 1953: sweets

September 1953: sugar and eggs

May 1954: butter, margarine and cheese

July 1954: bacon and meat – the last items to come off the ration.

National Service

As well as rationing, 1950s Britain faced another legacy of World War II: National Service. Young men still received call-up papers from the Ministry of Defence requiring them to join the armed forces and be prepared to fight if needed.

- **How old were the men who did National Service?** Most were 18 or 19.

- **How long did they do National Service for?** Between 18 and 24 months.

- **What training did they get?** Recruits learned to march in step and carry out drill moves with their rifles. This was called 'square-bashing', as most parade grounds were squares inside the barracks. The sergeant in charge inspected them regularly.

- **Did they do any fighting?** National Servicemen saw action in Korea, Kenya and Malaya. They were sent to guard the Suez Canal, Egypt, and patrol the deserts of Aden (in present-day Yemen).

- **When did National Service end?** The last recruits were called up in 1960 and discharged in 1963.

The swinging sixties

The end of National Service in 1960 had a dramatic effect on the nation's young men. Now that 18- and 19-year-olds didn't have to worry about being conscripted into the armed forces, they were free to break out of their fathers' mould and do their own thing.

One thing they didn't have to put up with any more was an army short-back-and-sides haircut. Instead, young men began to grow their hair long – a sign of rebelliousness against their parents' generation, and against authority.

All across the nation, young people began to dress the way they wanted. A flourishing fashion industry developed, with London's King's Road and Carnaby Street leading the way. The 1960s was the decade of the miniskirt, denim jeans, T-shirts and flowery shirts with big collars.

It was also the decade when Britain's music industry conquered the world with bands such as the Beatles and the Rolling Stones.

England: World Cup winners!

In July 1966, the football World Cup was held in England for the first time. The home team made it through to the final, played at Wembley Stadium, London, on 30 July.

In front of 98,000 spectators England beat West Germany 4–2 after extra time, and England captain Bobby Moore was presented with the solid-gold Jules Rimet trophy by Queen Elizabeth II. It was the first – and so far only – time that the nation which gave football to the world has succeeded in winning the world's greatest football competition.

Stolen!

The Jules Rimet trophy was stolen from a display in London in March 1966. It was found 7 days later – wrapped in newspaper underneath a garden hedge in South Norwood, London – by Pickles, a black and white collie dog.

The thief was never caught.

Times of change

If the 1960s had been a decade of 'anything goes', the 1970s was the decade when the lights went out – literally.

It started with a change that left many people feeling confused, when Britain's currency went decimal. Out went centuries of pounds, shillings and pence (based on counting in twenties and twelves), to be replaced by pounds and pence (based on counting in tens).

Decimal currency of 1971

Decimal Day or D-Day was 15 February 1971. On that day Britain changed from the centuries-old tradition of using 12 pence to the shilling and 20 shillings to the pound to a decimal system of 100 pence to the pound.

Pre-decimal coins: halfpenny, penny, 3 pence, 6 pence, shilling, florin (= 2 shillings), half-crown (2 shillings and 6 pence)

New decimal coins: halfpenny (discontinued 1983), penny, 2 pence, 5 pence, 10 pence, 50 pence.

Strikes and blackouts

In an echo of the 1920s, the early 1970s saw an unsettled period of industrial action. When the coalminers began a nationwide strike in January 1972, it didn't take long before power stations ran out of coal and electricity supplies were cut. Factories went onto a 3-day week to save power, and households got used to nightly blackouts and living by candlelight.

Britain in Europe

On 1 January 1973 Britain joined the European Economic Community (EEC), known today as the European Union (EU). For a nation so often at odds with the countries of Europe (particularly France and Germany) it was a big step to take, and many people felt it would weaken Britain and damage links with the countries of the Commonwealth.

Britain's membership of the EEC was put to the test in 1975, when the public voted two to one in favour of staying in Europe.

Northern Ireland

Northern Ireland was on everyone's mind in the 1970s. As far back as the 13th century England had sought to control Ireland – all of it. By the 1650s two thirds of all Irish land was owned or occupied by English Protestants. Many Irish saw the English as colonisers.

An Irish uprising in 1798 failed, leading, in 1801, to Britain and Ireland being united under one parliament and one flag. Ireland was now ruled from London, and the combined realm was called the United Kingdom of Great Britain and Ireland.

Fast forward to Easter 1916, when Irish nationalists proclaimed the formation of the Irish Republic. The Easter Rising was brutally ended by British soldiers, but it was the launchpad for what was to come.

In 1922, 26 of Ireland's 32 counties were granted self-rule as the Irish Free State, which, in 1949, became the Republic of Ireland.

However, Ireland's six northern counties opted to remain part of the United Kingdom. While this suited the Protestants, it didn't please the Catholics, who wanted freedom from Britain, like their counterparts in the south.

The Troubles

In the late 1960s, increased tension between the Catholic and Protestant communities of Northern Ireland led to violence. It was the start of a period which became known as 'the Troubles'.

The campaign of violence spread to England, and from the 1970s to the 1990s bombings were carried out by the Provisional wing of the Irish Republican Army (IRA). In 1984 an attempt was made by the IRA to assassinate British prime minister Margaret Thatcher by planting a bomb in her hotel in Brighton.

Towards peace

The IRA declared a ceasefire in 1994, enabling the Good Friday Agreement to be made in 1998. This was a peace agreement between Northern Ireland, the United Kingdom and the Republic of Ireland. Some powers were devolved from London to a new Northern Ireland Assembly, based in the Parliament Buildings in Belfast.

Northern Ireland

Republic of Ireland

The Winter of Discontent

As the 1970s drew to an end more strikes threatened Britain, and when lorry drivers, dustmen, health service workers and many others walked out during the winter of 1978–1979, rubbish piled up, the dead went unburied in Liverpool and Tameside, and schools were forced to close. A newspaper headline called it the 'Winter of Discontent'.

Summer of riots

In May 1979, Margaret Thatcher became Britain's first woman prime minister, and the nation embarked an an eventful 11 years.

The summer of 1981 saw rioting on the streets of English cities, resulting in arson, looting and violence. The riots were due to rising unemployment and racial tension between police and local communities.

10 April: Brixton riot, London
3 July: Toxteth riot, Liverpool
9 July: Sheffield riot
10 July: Handsworth riot, Birmingham
11 July: Chapeltown riot, Leeds

The Falklands War

On 2 April 1982, the people of Britain woke up to the news that the Falkland Islands – a British colony in the South Atlantic – had been invaded by Argentina, who claimed the islands were theirs, not Britain's.

A Royal Navy task force sailed to the Falklands, 8,000 miles (13,000 km) from Britain, on the biggest military operation of its kind since World War II.

The nation held its breath and watched as TV cameras filmed air strikes, damaged warships and British soldiers 'yomping' (marching with full kit) across the windswept islands. And when Argentina surrendered and the Union Jack was raised on 14 June, the nation had something to briefly take its mind off the troubles at home.

Unlike the century's two world wars, the Falklands War could do nothing to halt the rising tide of unemployment, and by 1983 some 4 million people were out of work. The scene was set for a battle of wills.

'Coal not dole'

The coalminers' strike of 1984 turned into the bitterest strike for a generation, sparked by the announcement of pit closures and job cuts.

By mid-March, 153 of the nation's 174 pits were on strike but, unlike the miners' strike of 1972, this time the government was prepared. Coal stocks had been built up and the lights stayed on. After a year, the strike failed and the miners were forced back to work. Prime Minister Thatcher hailed it as a 'major victory'.

The 'Battle of Orgreave'

Date: 18 June 1984

Location: Orgreave, South Yorkshire

What happened? Thousands of miners clashed with police in a series of running fights outside a coking plant, where coal was turned into coke for use in steel production. At one point, police on horses charged into the miners.

1987: A very stormy year

In the early hours of 16 October 1987, southern England was hit by hurricane-force winds – the worst storm to hit the country in almost 300 years. An estimated 15 million trees were blown over, buildings were damaged, power lines were brought down and several people were killed.

Three days later, on 19 October, a financial storm rocked the London Stock Exchange when £50 billion was wiped off the value of shares. This was 'Black Monday' but, unlike the stock-market crash of 50 years earlier, it was, thankfully, not the trigger for another Great Depression. It did, however, signal an end to the boom times of the 1980s – a decade in which nationalised industries were sold off and privatised, and financial services became the most imortant sector of the economy.

And when Prime Minister Thatcher resigned in November 1990, a controversial era in British politics came to an end.

Cool Britannia

The 1990s was a decade of increased pride in Britain and British culture, summed up by the catchphrase 'Cool Britannia'. It was a pun on 'Rule, Britannia', aimed at promoting Britain to a worldwide audience through the contemporary pop culture of bands such as Oasis, Blur, Pulp and the Spice Girls. And, while Britpop was blaring from the world's speakers, Britart was drawing in the crowds to the world's art galleries and auction houses, who couldn't get enough of the nation's Young British Artists, as they were known.

The optimistic feeling spilled over into the world of politics when, in 1997, Britain voted for a change of government to 'New Labour'. But, as one century ended and another began, the feel-good factor faded and Cool Britannia became a mere footnote in history.

The opening years of the 21st century saw Britain fighting unpopular wars in Iraq and Afghanistan, and when the financial markets suffered their worst crisis since the 1930s, a new era of austerity began.

Queen for 60 years

In 2012 Queen Elizabeth II celebrated her Diamond Jubilee – 60 years a queen. Only one other British monarch has reached this milestone: her great-great-grandmother, Queen Victoria, in 1897. Should Queen Elizabeth still be reigning on 9 September 2015, she will become Britain's longest-reigning monarch ever, at 63 years 217 days.

London Games, 2012

London was host city of both the 2012 Summer Olympics and the Paralympic Games. Great Britain finished third in both medal tables:

	Gold	Silver	Bronze
Olympics	29	17	19
Paralympics	34	43	43

This was the best British gold medal tally at any Olympics for 104 years. Each medal was 3.3 in (85 mm) in diameter and ¼ in (7mm) thick, but not since the Olympics of 1912 have solid gold medals been awarded. Instead, the modern 'gold' medal is gold-plated silver with a pinch of copper – but it must contain a minimum 0.2oz (6 g) of gold.

To the future and beyond

Like all histories, this one has no end. It began with the joining of nations to create a united kingdom but now, a little over 200 years later, the process of devolution in the United Kingdom has begun.

Power has been devolved or transferred from the UK Parliament in London to separate authorities in Scotland, Wales and Northern Ireland. Devolution is designed to decentralise government and give more power and freedom to these three nations which, together with England, make up the UK.

What does devolution mean for England? It means the dismantling of centuries of control by one nation over its neighbours, and it leaves England as the only part of the union not to have its own parliament.

This is the 'English question', and only the years ahead will provide ways of answering it.

How we live today

What's it like to live in Britain today? On the one hand, a large slice of the population seems to be afflicted with 'gadgetmania' as they upgrade to the latest must-have smartphone, tablet or HD TV. But, on the other hand, poverty is now a real and genuine concern for many, as personal debt rises and food handouts become a necessity.

Another way to view the state of the nation is with a few statistics:

- People are now living longer than ever before. Children born in 2009 can expect to live 20 years longer than those born in 1930: males to more than 78 years, females to more than 82 years.

- In 2010 there were 25.3 million houses in the UK – 9 million more than in 1961 and 1.4 million more since 2001.

- In 2010 adults in the UK aged 16 and over spent an average of 3.5 hours a day watching television, 2.5 hours using a computer and 1 hour listening to the radio.

- In 2010 there were a total of 34 million vehicles licensed in the UK, an increase of 4.2 million (14 per cent) since the end of 2001.

Royal reigns

Kings and queens of the United Kingdom

This is a complete list of monarchs since the creation of the United Kingdom in 1707. Earlier kings and queens of England are listed in Volumes 1 and 2.

- **House of Stuart**
1707–1714 Anne (queen of England since 1702)

- **House of Hanover**
1714–1727 George I
1727–1760 George II
1760–1820 George III
1820–1830 George IV
1830–1837 William IV
1837–1901 Victoria

- **House of Wettin (Saxe-Coburg-Gotha)**
1901–1910 Edward VII

- **House of Windsor**
1910–1936 George V
1936 Edward VIII
1936–1952 George VI
1952–present Elizabeth II

Britain's prime ministers

1721–1741	Sir Robert Walpole	Whig
1742	Spencer Compton	Whig
1743–1753	Henry Pelham	Whig
1754–1755	Thomas Pelham-Holles	Whig
1756	William Cavendish	Whig
1757–1761	Thomas Pelham-Holles	Whig
1762	John Stuart	Tory
1763–1764	George Grenville	Whig
1765	Charles Watson-Wentworth	Whig
1766	William Pitt the Elder	Whig
1767–1769	Augustus Fitzroy	Whig
1770–1781	Frederick North	Tory
1782	William FitzMaurice	Whig
1783	William Bentinck	Tory
1784–1800	William Pitt the Younger	Tory
1801–1803	Henry Addington	Tory
1804–1805	William Pitt the Younger	Tory
1806	William Grenville	Whig
1807–1808	William Bentinck	Tory
1809–1811	Spencer Perceval	Tory
1812–1826	Robert Jenkinson	Tory
1827	Frederick Robinson	Tory
1828–1829	Arthur Wellesley	Tory
1830–1833	Charles Grey	Whig
1834	Sir Robert Peel	Tory
1835–1840	William Lamb	Whig
1841–1845	Sir Robert Peel	Tory
1846–1851	Lord John Russell	Whig
1852	Edward Stanley	Conservative
1853–1854	George Hamilton-Gordon	Con
1855–1864	Viscount Palmerston	Liberal
1865	John Russell	Lib

1866–1867	Edward Stanley	Con
1868	Benjamin Disraeli	Con
1869–1873	William Ewart Gladstone	Lib
1874–1879	Benjamin Disraeli	Con
1880–1884	William Ewart Gladstone	Lib
1885	Marquess of Salisbury	Con
1886	William Ewart Gladstone	Lib
1887–1891	Marquess of Salisbury	Con
1892–1893	William Ewart Gladstone	Lib
1894	Earl of Rosebery	Lib
1895–1901	Marquess of Salisbury	Con
1902–1904	Arthur Balfour	Con
1905–1907	Henry Campbell-Bannerman	Lib
1908–1915	Herbert H. Asquith	Lib
1916–1921	David Lloyd George	Lib
1922	Andrew Bonar Law	Con
1923–1928	Stanley Baldwin	Con
1929–1934	James Ramsay MacDonald	Labour
1935–1936	Stanley Baldwin	Con
1937–1939	Neville Chamberlain	Con
1940–1944	Winston Churchill	Con
1945–1950	Clement Attlee	Lab
1951–1954	Winston Churchill	Con
1955–1956	Sir Anthony Eden	Con
1957–1962	Harold Macmillan	Con
1963	Sir Alec Douglas-Home	Con
1964–1969	Harold Wilson	Lab
1970–1973	Edward Heath	Con
1974–1975	Harold Wilson	Lab
1976–1978	James Callaghan	Lab
1979–1989	Margaret Thatcher	Con
1990–1996	John Major	Con
1997–2006	Tony Blair	Lab
2007–2009	Gordon Brown	Lab
2010–	David Cameron	Con

Glossary

abdicate To give up the throne; to resign from the position of monarch.

austerity A time of economic and financial hardship.

Blitz The bombing of British towns and cities during World War II; from the German word for 'lightning'.

Bow Street Runners An early police force in London.

cholera A life-threatening disease caught by drinking contaminated water.

coalition A pact or treaty made by individuals or groups who join together for a common purpose.

conscription Compulsory enlistment ('calling up') to serve in the armed forces.

Corn Laws Laws designed to protect the market for home-grown corn by restricting the amount of foreign corn that could be imported into Britain.

decimalisation The process of converting to decimal currency, based on multiples of 10.

demobilise To take troops out of active service, usually at the end of a war.

emigrate To leave one country in order to live in another.

Luddite A person who destroyed factory machines in the belief that they were doing workers out of their jobs; named after Ned Ludd, an imaginary weaver.

Martello tower A small defensive fort.

middle class The social group between the upper and working classes.

nationalisation The process of taking a privately run industry into public (government) ownership.

National Service Compulsory service in the armed forces during peacetime.

navvies Labourers who built the canal and railway networks; from the word 'navigator'.

penal colony A settlement for prisoners in a remote location far away from their homes.

radical A person who calls for political or social reform.

rationing The restriction of goods during a time of crisis, such as a war.

rotten borough An election district having only a few voters but the same voting power as other, more populous districts.

suffragette A woman seeking the right to vote through organised protest.

Swing Riots A series of riots by farm workers; named after Captain Swing, an imaginary character.

trade union An organisation of workers united to protect and promote their common interests.

transportation A punishment in which offenders were forcibly sent (transported) to lands overseas, such as Australia.

upper class The social group that has the highest status in society, especially the aristocracy.

welfare state A system whereby the government protects the health and wellbeing of its citizens.

working class The social group consisting of people who are employed for wages, especially in manual or industrial work.

Yeomanry A volunteer cavalry force raised from men who held and cultivated small estates of land.

yomping A military term for marching long distances with full kit.

A modern England timeline

1801 The United Kingdom of Great Britain and Ireland is formed when Ireland joins the UK.

1803 Napoleon Bonaparte plans to invade England from France.

1805 Bonaparte's invasion of England is called off. Battle of Trafalgar: the combined French and Spanish fleets are defeated by the Royal Navy.

1807 Slave trade is abolished in the British Empire.

1811–1816 Luddites destroy machines and factories.

1815 Battle of Waterloo: Bonaparte's French army is defeated.

1816 Spa Fields riot, London, fails to overthrow the government.

1819 A peaceful meeting in Manchester turns into the Peterloo Massacre when soldiers kill 11 people.

1820 George III dies and is succeeded by George IV. The Cato Street Conspiracy fails to overthrow the government.

1825 Stockton to Darlington railway opens.

1830 George IV dies and is succeeded by William IV. Liverpool and Manchester railway opens.

1830–1831 The Swing Riots, when farm workers in the south of England smash threshing machines.

1831 First cholera epidemic.

1832 The Reform Act marks a major advance in parliamentary democracy.

1833 The Factory Act improves working conditions for children. Six farm workers from Tolpuddle, Dorset, are transported to Australia for forming a union.

1833 Slavery is abolished in much of the British Empire.

1834 The Palace of Westminster, London, burns down. The Poor Law Amendment Act creates parish workhouses for the poor.

1837 William IV dies and is succeeded by Victoria. Euston opens as first London railway station.

1840 World's first stamp, the Penny Black, is issued.

1841 First excursion by railway.

1846 Corn Laws abolished.

1850 Britain's first free public library opens.

1851 Great Exhibition in the Crystal Palace, London.

1854–1856 The Crimean War.

1859 Big Ben's first strike.

1868 The last public hanging.

1871 First Bank Holiday; first international rugby match, Scotland vs. England.

1872 First FA Cup Final; first international football match, Scotland vs. England.

1887 Golden Jubilee of Queen Victoria's reign.

1888 Football League is formed.

1897 Diamond Jubilee of Queen Victoria's reign.

1899–1902 The Boer War.

1901 Queen Victoria dies and is succeeded by Edward VII.

1903 Suffragette movement is formed.

1908 First London Olympics.

1910 Edward VII dies and is succeeded by George V.

1913 Death of suffragette Emily Davison at the Epsom Derby.

1914–1918 World War I.

1917 The Royal Family's surname is changed from Saxe-Coburg-Gotha to Windsor.

1918 Women aged 30 and over have the right to vote.

1918–1919 'Spanish' flu kills tens of thousands.

1922 Ireland gains independence from the United Kingdom. BBC founded.

1924–1925 The British Empire Exhibition.

1926 The General Strike.

1928 The voting age for women is lowered to 21, the same as for men.

1929 First BBC television transmission.

1929–1930s The Great Depression.

1932 The National Hunger March.

1936 George V dies and is succeeded by Edward VIII, who abdicates and is succeeded by George VI. The Jarrow March. The Crystal Palace burns down.

1939–1945 World War II.

1940 Adolf Hitler plans to invade England; the Battle of Britain; British cities are bombed in the Blitz; food rationing is introduced.

1942 The Beveridge Report lays the foundations for the Welfare State.

1945–1951 A period of austerity.

1948 The National Health Service begins. Industries are nationalised. Second London Olympics.

1951 Festival of Britain.

1952 George VI dies and is succeeded by Elizabeth II.

1953 Coronation of Elizabeth II.

1954 Rationing ends.

1955 ITV begins television transmissions.

1959 The Mini car goes on sale.

1960 National Service ends.

1966 The football World Cup is staged in England, and the host nation wins the tournament.

1969 Supersonic airliner Concorde makes its maiden flight. Capital punishment abolished.

1970s Dutch Elm Disease destroys Britain's elm trees.

1971 Britain's currency is decimalised.

1972 The three-day week, power cuts and blackouts.

1973 Britain joins the EEC.

1974 IRA begins bombing campaign in English towns.

1977 Silver Jubilee of Queen Elizabeth's reign.

1978–1979 The 'Winter of Discontent'.

1981 Rioting on the streets of towns and cities.

1982 The Falklands War.

1984 The miners' strike. Assassination attempt by IRA on Prime Minister Margaret Thatcher in Brighton.

1985 Live Aid concert at Wembley Stadium, London.

1987 'Black Monday' stock market crash. Hurricane-force storm wreaks havoc across southern England.

1989 The Hillsborough Disaster, Sheffield, in which 96 Liverpool FC supporters died in an accidental crush during a football match.

1990 The Poll Tax riot, London.

1991 IRA mortar bombs fired at 10 Downing Street.

1992 Windsor Castle is damaged by fire.

1994 The Channel Tunnel opens between Britain and France.

1996 An IRA bomb devastates Manchester city centre.

2002 Golden Jubilee of Queen Elizabeth's reign.

2003 England win the rugby World Cup.

2005 Suicide bombers bring terror to London.

2008 A worldwide financial crisis affects British banks.

2011 Rioting on the streets of towns and cities.

2012 London Olympics and Paralympics. Diamond Jubilee of Queen Elizabeth's reign.

Index

Other volumes in this set:

England: A Very Peculiar History

Volume 1: From Ancient Times to Agincourt

by David Arscott ISBN: 978-1-908973-37-5

Introduction: A mongrel race

Volume 2: From the Wars of the Roses to the Industrial Revolution

by Ian Graham ISBN: 978-1-908973-38-2

Introduction: Turbulent times

The Cherished Library

Edited by Stephen Haynes

A CLASSIFIED LIST
OF THE FIRST 43 VOLUMES

Available in hardback binding
and for all digital platforms

Very Peculiar Histories™

History of the British Isles
England (in 3 volumes)
  Vol. 1: From Ancient Times to Agincourt
    David Arscott   978-1-908973-37-5
  Vol. 2: From the Wars of the Roses to the
    Industrial Revolution *Ian Graham*   978-1-908973-38-2
  Vol. 3: From Trafalgar to the New Elizabethans
    John Malam   978-1-908973-39-9
  Boxed set of all three volumes: 978-1-908973-41-2
Scotland (in 2 volumes) *Fiona Macdonald*
  Vol. 1: From Ancient Times to Robert the Bruce
                  978-1-906370-91-6
  Vol. 2: From the Stewarts to Modern Scotland
                  978-1-906714-79-6
Ireland *Jim Pipe*   978-1-905638-98-7
Wales *Rupert Matthews*   978-1-907184-19-2

History of the 20th century
Titanic *Jim Pipe*   978-1-907184-87-1
World War One *Jim Pipe*   978-1-908177-00-1
World War Two *Jim Pipe*   978-1-908177-97-1
The Blitz *David Arscott*   978-1-907184-18-5
Rations *David Arscott*   978-1-907184-25-3
The 60s *David Arscott*   978-1-908177-92-6

Social history
Victorian Servants *Fiona Macdonald*   978-1-907184-49-9

North of the Border
Scottish Clans *Fiona Macdonald*   978-1-908759-90-0
Scottish Tartan and Highland Dress
 Fiona Macdonald   978-1-908759-89-4
Scottish Words *Fiona Macdonald*   978-1-908759-63-4
Whisky *Fiona Macdonald*   978-1-907184-76-5

British places
Brighton *David Arscott*   978-1-906714-89-5
London *Jim Pipe*   978-1-907184-26-0
Yorkshire *John Malam*   978-1-907184-57-4

Myths and legends

This is Volume 43 of The Cherished Library. A list of authors and their works in this series will be found on the preceding pages. The publishers will be pleased to send freely to all applicants an illustrated catalogue of the Library and our many other publications.

Book House
25 Marlborough Place
Brighton
BN1 1UB

www.salariya.com

Some reviews of other volumes in this series

Rations by David Arscott

'Excellent little book bringing back many memories, some good and some not so good.'

Rolie

Christmas by Fiona Macdonald

'Perfect to dip in and out of and an ideal stocking filler. . . . Plenty of ideas to talk about with your family and friends . . . enchanting little book.'

Parents in Touch